SHAWN MacLachlan

A BRONTOSAUR
the life story unearthed

BEVERLY HALSTEAD D.Sc.
(Reader in Geology and Zoology, Reading University)

pictures by
JENNY HALSTEAD

COLLINS

William Collins Sons & Co Ltd
London · Glasgow · Sydney · Auckland
Toronto · Johannesburg

First published 1982
© text Beverly Halstead 1982
© illustrations Jenny Halstead 1982
ISBN 0 00 104111 8
Made and printed in Great Britain by
William Collins Sons & Co Ltd Glasgow

Introduction

The dinosaur on which this story is based lived some 150 million years ago during the Upper Jurassic period and was discovered in rocks of the Morrison Formation in the State of Utah, U.S.A., but many other similar dinosaurs have been found in the State of Colorado and in Europe. The first scientific description was written by O.C. Marsh of Yale University in 1877, and he gave the name *Apatosaurus ajax* to an almost complete skeleton. This type of dinosaur is popularly known as *Brontosaurus*, or Thunder Lizard.

Apatosaurus ajax would have weighed about three kilos at birth, the weight of a newborn human baby, but would have grown to an enormous thirty tonnes, and about twenty-two metres long. Sections of the leg bones show annual growth rings and up to 120 have been counted.

Footprints show that *Apatosaurus* had a big pad on each foot to take his great weight. He also had one claw and four small hooves on his front feet, and three claws and two hooves on his back feet. The claws would help him to grip on soft ground. Footprints also show the ripping claws of flesh-eating dinosaurs who would almost certainly have attacked young brontosaurs.

This story tells of one brontosaur, *Apatosaurus ajax*, whom we have called Ajax.

The warm sand surrounded the eggs which were nearly ready to hatch. Faint taps could be heard and several of the shells began to crack. Baby brontosaurs poked their heads out into the glaring sunlight. They rolled over, out of their eggs and onto the sand. Their first instinct was to find shade. Suddenly they were overshadowed by dark shapes, and leathery-winged pterosaurs with fearsome beaks swooped down on the newly hatched dinosaurs to feast on them. A few stumbled away to reach the safety of the dark undergrowth and so escaped the onslaught.

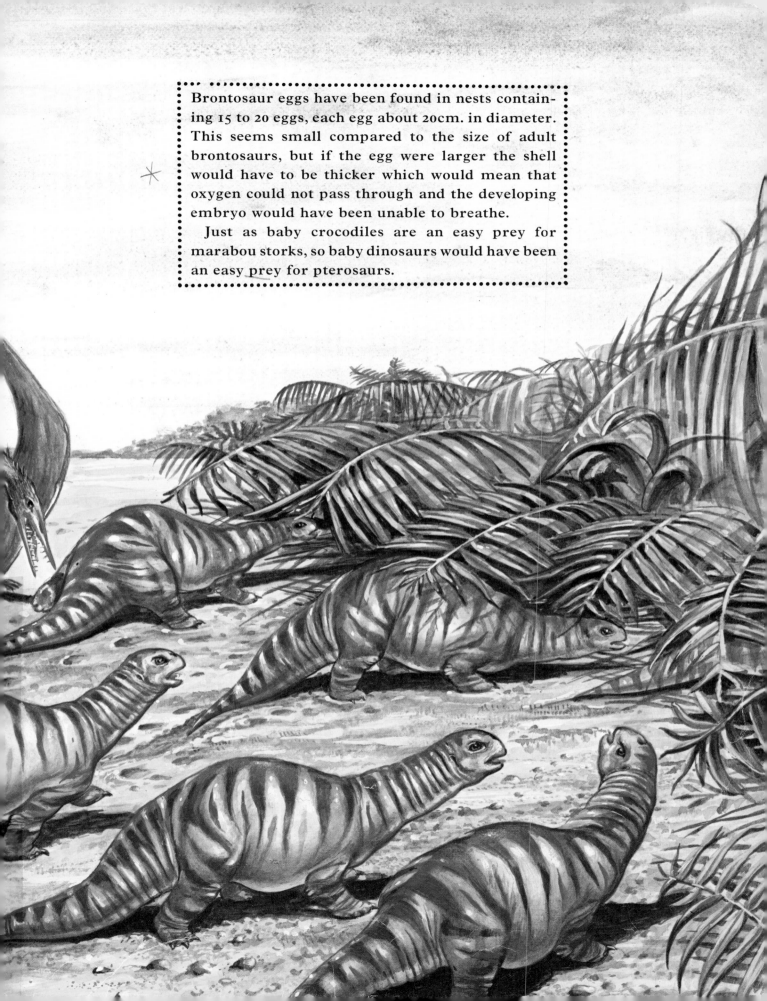

Brontosaur eggs have been found in nests containing 15 to 20 eggs, each egg about 20cm. in diameter. This seems small compared to the size of adult brontosaurs, but if the egg were larger the shell would have to be thicker which would mean that oxygen could not pass through and the developing embryo would have been unable to breathe.

Just as baby crocodiles are an easy prey for marabou storks, so baby dinosaurs would have been an easy prey for pterosaurs.

Two of the young dinosaurs who fled into the undergrowth stayed close to each other. They ate small insects and soft juicy leaves. Bright green lizards flashed past them. Occasionally a bird with a long tail, *Archaeopteryx*, glided down and chased the dinosaurs along the ground. Sometimes it climbed tree trunks, using the three claws on the front of its wings.

At night, when the dinosaurs were sleeping, small furry shrew-like mammals came out of the undergrowth to hunt for beetles and worms.

We know what else lived at the same time as these brontosaurs because of the fossil remains found buried in the rocks, and we can tell the age of the rocks by radioactivity. The other creatures found include other dinosaurs, the flying pterosaurs, *Archaeopteryx*, lizards, small mammals, even owls, beetles and centipedes; among the ferns were the first true flowering plants such as *Magnolia*.

One day, when the young brontosaurs were browsing in a glade in the forest, they were suddenly surprised by three long-legged meat-eating dinosaurs, *Coelurus*. The carnivores pounced on the

nearest of the young brontosaurs, tearing him open with their strong claws to feast upon him. The surviving brontosaur, Ajax, escaped into the undergrowth, as fast as he could.

Ajax, wandered on and on, intent on only one thing: food. For he was growing bigger all the time. His dusty skin began to peel and a brighter shiny one appeared. His neck became longer and this made it easier for him to reach higher for young leaves. Sometimes he was forced to eat older, tougher plants which were difficult to digest. One day, on his wanderings, he came to a dried-up river bed. Here he found many rounded pebbles, which he picked up in his mouth and swallowed. In this way Ajax acquired his first set of stomach stones. Now, when he was forced to eat tough, fibrous plants the stones pounded the fibres in his stomach, making them easier to digest.

While he was intently collecting pebbles a small herd of *Hypsilophodon* entered the clearing. Soon they were all round him, grazing contentedly off the plants. When Ajax looked up he started, and lashed his tail as a warning in case they were flesh-eaters who would attack him. But instead they bounded away from him into the forest.

> We cannot be sure about the colouring as it is not preserved, but it is reasonable to assume that when small, brontosaurs were patterned for protective camouflage, and as they grew their skin gradually faded and turned grey as they aged.
>
> We can be certain the brontosaur was a plant eater from its teeth, and sometimes plant remains are preserved in the stomach. Fossils have revealed highly polished stones in the stomach region their function is believed to be the same as stomach stones found in crocodiles.

Ajax roamed through the forest, eating and growing. Years
passed. One year during the rainy season there was a tremendous
storm. The wind tore through the forest, bringing tall trees
crashing to the ground. Everything was swaying and branches
were flying through the air. A jagged streak of lightning lit the
sky, followed immediately by a resounding crack of thunder.
Then the skies opened and torrents of rain poured down.

Ajax ran to escape the torrential downpour, the crashing trees,
the lightning and the cracking thunder, more terrifying than
volcanic eruptions. He ran and ran, not knowing where he was
going, until eventually the storm abated and he fell down,
exhausted, to sleep.

When Ajax woke he was no longer in the forest he had known all his life. There were fewer trees and less shade. He ambled along, feeding as he went. Then he reached the edge of the forest. There, before him, was an open plain. Grazing in the distance were herds of dinosaurs, *Camptosaurus*.

For some time he stayed near the edge of the forest. Then, cautiously, he ventured further and further out across the flat plain. Ahead, the plants were a deeper green colour which he knew meant lush, tender food.

From fossilized wood and plant remains we know what the landscape was like: the forests and plains, the muddy swamps full of dinosaur footprints.

Ajax moved slowly across the vast plain, and found himself
in the swamps at the edge of a lake. He waded into the water and
began pulling up plants and scooping mouthfuls of water weed.
On nearby sandbanks small groups of squat, heavily-armoured
Acanthopholis peacefully chewed horsetails. Blue dragonflies
hovered over the water or clung to the weed.

    This was an ideal place. Suddenly Ajax saw what looked like
two scaly logs moving fast towards him. Their speed increased as
they closed in on him. Their huge mouths opened. He quickly

lifted his head out of the water, turned his body round as fast as possible and lashed with his tail. The two crocodiles moved off, after smaller and easier prey.

Ajax's great size means his skin would have got very hot during the day, and he would, therefore, want to spend many hours wallowing in water to keep cool. The nostril on the top of the head is a sign of an air breather that spends a lot of time in water.

Some time later Ajax was wandering over a sandy hillside when he heard a piercing scream. He hurried towards the sound and saw a dinosaur like himself being attacked by a fierce flesh-eater, *Ceratosaurus*. Ajax rushed towards the attacker, lashing his tail. The suddenness of his onslaught made the *Ceratosaurus* pause, and Ajax crashed his tail across its back. The *Ceratosaurus* turned and fled, leaving the two brontosaurs standing side by side. Only then did Ajax feel the sharp pain in his tail. It had broken.

Now Ajax had a companion, a young female brontosaur. If they stayed together they would be safer from attacks by flesh-eaters. Ajax's tail gradually healed, but he always had a thick, bony lump where the broken bones had grown together again.

Of the many skeletons of brontosaur excavated one had a large bony lump on its tail, showing that it had been fractured during life. This specimen is in the Wellcome Medical collection in the Science Museum, London.

Ajax and his companion spent their days feeding and wading in the swamps, until they gradually reached the open lakes, where they met other brontosaurs. As they waded deeper into the water they found they were able to swim, pawing the bottom with their front feet. With their bodies under water they could breathe easily with their heads just poking above the surface.

Evidence that these dinosaurs could swim comes from fossil footprints in the Paluxy River, Texas, where there are trackways showing only front footprints, with an occasional back footprint where they put it down to turn and swim in another direction. As they could not have been walking on their front legs, they must have been swimming.

Months passed and Ajax and his companion stayed together. One day as they were feeding on the shores of the lake they saw a herd of dinosaurs like themselves moving through the trees at the edge of the forest. The two young dinosaurs walked across the flat marshy ground towards the forest. As they trampled the shrubs underfoot, clouds of insects rose and a flock of pterosaurs swooped down, snapping them up in their strong beaks.

When they reached the herd the giant lumbering adults allowed the two to join them, and together they all moved off, the younger ones protected by the larger adults.

Sometimes, when Ajax moved towards the head of the herd, one of the older males would hit him with his tail to make sure he kept to his place. Eventually the herd reached a large inlet where a series of streams entered a lake. Here the dinosaurs settled down and remained for many years. Here, too, Ajax grew to a mature adult.

Footprints show us that brontosaurs lived in herds, and when they were on the move the younger adults walked between the very large mature adults. There is no evidence of very young brontosaurs in these herds, so it is safe to assume they did not join a herd until nearly adult.

When Ajax was fully grown he several times challenged the leader of the herd. But each time he was firmly struck across the neck by the leader's tail and was forced to retreat.

One day, he stood his ground. This was the signal, and the rest of the herd drew away, leaving Ajax and the leader alone. The two dinosaurs stood side by side, head to tail, for this was the way they would fight. Each lashed his tail with all his strength at the other's neck. Ajax had the advantage: he was

younger and stronger and the bony lump on his tail gave him
added force. At last the leader weakened, dropped his neck, and
slowly backed away, defeated. Ajax was the leader of the herd.

This aspect of behaviour, fighting for leadership,
has been based on our observations of the activities
of tropical reptiles in their native habitat.

Together Ajax and his companion led the herd. Every spring the herd moved to the forests to feed on the new shoots, but spent most of the year around the creeks of the lake. And every spring in a shady patch of ground at the edge of the forest Ajax's mate and the other females in the herd laid their eggs. They covered

them with dead leaves and dry ferns before scraping a mound of sand over the nest. Then the eggs were left to hatch on their own.

Lots of fossil broken egg shells have been found by themselves. Occasionally an adult skeleton has been found close by.

After the herd had lived in and around the lake for several years, the water in the creeks began to dry up. No longer could the brontosaurs wallow in the shallow water and the food supply was insufficient for the herd. They had to move on.

Ajax, his mate and the stronger dinosaurs led the herd along dried-up river beds until they came to a vast desert. Far in the distance were cloud-covered hills. They knew if they were to find water they must cross the desert to reach the hilly area. So,

under a blazing sun, they set off. But it was a cruel journey. With no food and no water the older and weaker dinosaurs collapsed on the sand and were left behind to die. When they finally arrived at the hills the herd was half its size.

Fossilized remains of many early brontosaurs have been found in Western Europe in what was a 120km wide desert separating a hilly region from inland sea or large lake. Their death is presumed to have been caused by the conditions described.

When they came close to the hills, the dinosaurs found lakes and rivers, swamps and lush vegetation. Instead of keeping together the herd spread out, all hurrying to the shore for water and food. Suddenly a pack of giant *Allosaurus* appeared from the rocky ground and closed in on the scattered tired brontosaurs, surrounding them and tearing them to pieces. The remaining brontosaurs quickly formed a circle round the females and younger ones, but the flesh-eaters launched themselves on them, slashing and ripping the flanks of the herd with the dagger-like talons of their hind legs.

The brontosaurs lashed their tails at the attackers who eventually retreated and contented themselves by gorging the bodies of the brontosaurs they had already killed. At last the danger passed and Ajax led the few survivors to the safety of the lake. In this final battle many had been killed, including Ajax's companion and mate.

Gradually, as the years passed, the herd recovered its strength. Younger, more energetic dinosaurs grew up and Ajax found his leadership being challenged more often. The day came when once again the leadership was in dispute. A young male brontosaur stood his ground, despite severe blows from Ajax's tail. At last Ajax had no more energy for the fight. He lowered his head, turned and walked away from the herd for ever.

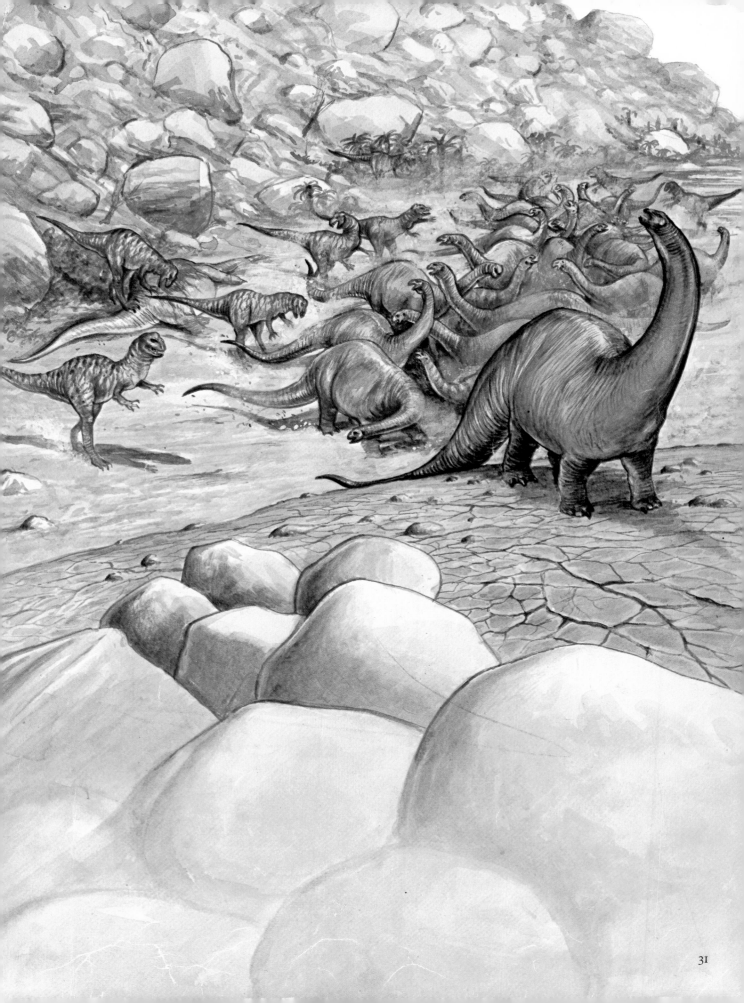

Ajax was 120 years old. He lay down in the warm sand. Nearby a nest of brontosaur eggs began to hatch. Hungry pterosaurs swooped down, but a sudden movement from Ajax's tail alarmed them and the hatchlings scuttled to safety. Ajax closed his eyes for the last time. All was still.

Eric Kincaid's
ANIMAL
CLASSICS

Eric Kincaid's
ANIMAL CLASSICS

retold by
GRAEME KENT

Illustrated by
ERIC KINCAID

Brimax Books·Newmarket·England

CONTENTS

ISBN 0 86112 495 2
© Brimax Books Ltd 1988. All rights reserved
Published by Brimax Books, Newmarket, England 1988
Printed in Hong Kong

INTRODUCTION

There are thousands of different kinds of animals on the face of the earth. Most of them have been the subjects of stories. Some of the best of these tales will be found in this book.

There are stories concerned with wild beasts at times of great action and excitement. A war-horse charges into battle, with shot and shell bursting about its ears. A hunter tracks down an African elephant, while a great white whale turns the tables on its pursuers and lures them to their doom. Explorers stumble across a terrifying prehistoric monster still roaming across the earth. One dog shows its love for its master by saving him from drowning.

Other stories in this collection deal with the most fantastic and incredible creatures ever to prowl through the pages of books. A cowardly lion hurries along a yellow brick road with a scarecrow and a tin woodman. A blind cat who can see, and a lame fox who can run, swindle a trusting puppet out of his money. A swallow heading for the warm lands as winter falls, stays to help a statue to assist others, and as a result freezes to death. Two important, dignified men find themselves changed into storks, forget how to transform themselves back again, and have to depend upon the wits of an unusual owl to effect the change.

There are many more animals here for our delight. A jumping frog loses a match because someone plays a trick on its owner. A shy dragon who hates fighting refuses a challenge from St George. A water baby who can talk to fish rescues a lobster from a trap.

The stories are set as far apart as Arabia and the Deep South of America; Kansas and Never-Never Land; the steamy jungles and vast oceans; battlefields and lonely moors. They are written by such masters as Kenneth Grahame, Oscar Wilde, Mark Twain, Andrew Lang and Sir Arthur Conan Doyle.

These fascinating stories show a huge variety of animals as they fly and swim, run and tunnel. They set out on remarkable journeys, have great adventures and meet incredible characters.

They are all here for us to enjoy.

THE JUMPING FROG

by Mark Twain

Jim Smiley was a miner. In the winter of 1850 he was working in one of the great gold-mining camps of the American West.

Now Jim was a nice fellow, but he had one great weakness. He would bet money on anything. If he couldn't get anyone to bet against him on one side, then he would change over and bet on the other side. Any way that suited the other man would do for Jim. He was happy as long as he could bet. It did not matter what he was betting on.

If there was a horse-race, Jim would be there with his money. If there was a dog-fight, Jim would back one of the dogs. If there were two birds sitting on a tree branch, Jim would put money on which one would fly off first. If he saw a bug moving, he would bet cash on how long it would take to get where it was going. Then he would follow it to make sure.

Once, when the parson's wife was ill, Jim being a kind-hearted fellow, went to see her.

"How are you?" he asked.

"The doctor says I'm going to get better," the lady said.

Jim thought for a moment. "Bet you two dollars that you don't," he said in the end.

Jim bought a horse. It was old, slow and broken down. It was a sorry sight. At first the other miners in the camp used to laugh at it. If they held a horse-race they would give Jim's nag a long start. Naturally Jim would bet on it to win. When the race began Jim's horse would be nowhere at all for a long time. Then, in the last few seconds, Jim's mare would get all excited and come racing up to win by a short head.

Next Jim bought himself a dog. It was a bull-pup. Like the horse it was not much to look at. It was small and thin and sad. Jim used to match his pup in fights against all the other dogs in the camp. In contest after contest the bull-pup would be tossed at first, all over the place.

The other miners would bet against Jim's dog. When all the money was down Jim would give a shout. His dog would seem to go crazy. He would hurl himself on the other dog in a flurry of snaps and bites until his foe turned and fled.

One day, however, the bull-pup met his match. The bull-pup's pet move was to bite at his enemy's hind legs. Then a gang of miners put the dog up against a mut that had no hind legs. They had been cut off in an accident with a saw.

Jim's dog loafed around until all the money had been bet. Then Jim gave his usual shout. At once the pup went for the other dog's hind legs. Only there weren't any. First the bull-pup looked surprised. Then he looked fed up. He gave Jim a stare, as if to say that his heart was broken. That look seemed to be saying it was all Jim's fault for putting up a dog that had no hind legs to get hold of. The bull-pup gave up and limped off. He was no good as a fighting dog after that.

On the whole, though, Jim seemed to have a lot of luck with his animals. He had tom cats, and terriers and fighting cocks. He entered them in all sorts of events, and more often than not they won. The miners said that Jim was lucky.

Jim must have thought so as well. But one day he pushed his luck too far. He got himself a frog.

He caught this frog and said he would train it. He took the frog to his tent and spent three months teaching it to jump.

Jim spent all his spare time on this. By the time he had finished that frog could perform like a circus acrobat. It became a champion at catching flies. No matter how far away the fly might be the frog would leap through the air and swallow it.

Jim called his frog Daniel Webster. Jim knew that all he had to do was call out "Flies, Daniel, flies!" and the frog would take off into the air. Then it would flop back down on to the floor again.

But what the frog really became famous for was leaping across the ground. Miners would come from miles around to see it jump. They would bet Jim that the frog could not jump a certain distance. Jim would put up his money and then, as sure as fate, the frog would soar across the space.

Jim used to keep Daniel Webster in a box he had made. One day a stranger came to the camp. He saw Jim with the box, and said:

"What might it be that you've got in that box?"

"It might be a parrot, or it might be a canary," Jim said, "but it ain't – it's only just a frog."

The fellow looked in the box.

"Hmm, so it is," he said. "Well, what's he good for?"

"I'll tell you," said Jim. "He's good for one thing. He can out-jump any frog in this county."

The fellow took the box again, and had another long look, and gave it back to Jim.

"I don't see no points about that frog that's better than any other frog."

"Maybe you don't," Jim said. "Maybe you know about frogs and maybe you don't. Anyway, I've got my opinion. I'll bet forty dollars that he can jump farther than any other frog in the county."

The man thought for a moment, and then said sadly, "Well, I'm only a stranger here, and I ain't got no frog; but if I had a frog I'd bet you."

At once Jim said, "That's all right. If you'll hold my box a minute, I'll go and get you a frog."

The man took the box, and put his forty dollars down next to Jim's, and sat down to wait.

He waited on his own for some time, and then he had an idea. He reached into his pocket and took out a handful of small metal pellets used for shooting ducks.

Then he took Jim's frog out of the box. He opened its mouth. Carefully he poured the shot into the frog, filling him almost up to his chin.

Jim was still out in the swamp looking for another frog. He had to slop around in the mud for a long time, but finally he found one and took it in and gave it to the man.

"Now, if you're ready," he said, "put your frog next to Daniel Webster. I'll give you the word to start."

The two men put the frogs on the ground, side by side.

"One-two-three-jump!" said Jim.

Both men touched their frogs from behind. The new frog hopped off. Daniel Webster, weighed down by all the shot that had been shovelled into him, gave a heave, but he could not move. He was planted as solid as an anvil.

17

Jim was surprised and disgusted, but of course he had no idea what was the matter with Daniel. The other fellow took the money. As he was going out of the door he jerked his thumb at Daniel Webster, and said:

"Well, I still don't see no points about that frog that's better than any other frog."

For a long time Jim stood scratching his head and looking down at Daniel Webster. The frog did not move.

"I do wonder why that frog didn't jump," said Jim. "I wonder if there ain't something wrong with him. He looks mighty baggy, somehow."

As he spoke he lifted Daniel Webster up.

"Why, blame my cats," he said. "He must weigh five pounds."

He turned the frog upside down. All the pellets of shot poured out of Daniel Webster's mouth. Jim was the maddest of men. He put the frog down and chased out after the other fellow, but he never caught him.

FOR THE LOVE OF A MAN

from "The Call of the Wild" – by Jack London

Buck was a sledge dog. Some said that he was the best in all the cold lands of the North, where men looked for gold.

It was his job to lead the other dogs who pulled the sledge of his master, John Thornton. Buck was given this job because he was braver and stronger than the rest.

Buck was a wild dog. He sat by John's fire at night, but he could still hear the call of the wild things from the great dark forest. When he fought he fought like a wild beast, with teeth and claws. He fought to the death. Kill, or be killed, it was the only law he knew.

He had won his place as the leader of the nine-dog team in a fierce fight. The chief dog before him had been Spitz, a strong white husky. As soon as Buck had joined the team Spitz had started to steal his food and to drive him away from the fire at night.

Buck had put up with this for a short time. Then he knew that he would have to fight Spitz, or starve to death.

The battle took place one evening on the hard-packed snow. As usual Spitz tried to drive Buck away from his food.

Buck did not cry out. He drove at Spitz, shoulder to shoulder. Both dogs rolled in the snow, Spitz on top. Twice his teeth clipped together, like the steel jaws of a trap. Buck pushed himself to his feet. In vain he tried to sink his teeth into the neck of the big white dog.

Time after time Buck rushed at his enemy. Spitz kept driving him back. Soon Buck was soaked in his own blood. He knew that he would not last much longer.

Now the other dogs were sure that Spitz would win. But Buck had one trick left. Again he rushed at Spitz, as if to hit him with his shoulder once more. At the last second he dived low, just above the snow. His teeth closed on the other dog's left front leg.

There was the crunch of a breaking bone, and the white dog faced Buck on three legs. Still Spitz fought on, but there was no hope for him. In another minute or so he lay dead on the snow. The team had a new lead dog.

There was only one living thing that Buck loved, and that was his master John. For months of each year John lived in a tent pitched on the snow between a forest of pine trees and a great frozen river. When the snow stopped falling and the wind dropped he would go out on his sledge, pulled by Buck and the other dogs. For day after day they would travel over the ice and snow while John looked for gold.

Buck adored his master. John looked after his dogs. After a day's work he would feed them with dried fish and then talk to them for hours. He would pat them and play with them.

Buck used to lie at his master's feet, looking up at his face as John spoke. When John moved about the camp, Buck would follow him, keeping close to the miner.

Twice in a short time Buck was able to save his master.

No other man meant anything to Buck. The other miners saw this one day in Clay City. John had made the long journey there to buy food.

After he had put his food away in his sledge, John went to the saloon for a drink. He took Buck with him. The dog lay on the floor, his chin on his paws. He did not take his eyes off his master.

It was then that 'Black' Burton, the bully of the city, came in. He was a big man with a quick temper.

Soon Burton started to pick a fight with a small man who stood at the bar. John tried to stop the bully. Burton hit him as hard as he could.

John was sent spinning. He held on to the bar to stop himself falling. Burton came towards him, his fist held high.

Then the other men in the bar heard a noise. It was not a bark, nor was it a yelp. It was more of a roar. They saw Buck's body rise up in the air as he left the floor. The dog sprang at Burton's throat.

The big man saved his life by putting up his arm. Then he fell to the floor, with the dog on top of him.

Buck took his teeth out of the bully's arm and went for his throat again. This time his teeth sank deep into Burton's neck.

The other miners managed to drive Buck off, but still he stood by the door, barking until he was sure that his master was safe.

The miners held a special meeting to make up their minds what to do about Buck. In the end, they said that the dog had done the right thing in helping his master. Burton should not have hit John in the saloon.

Not long after that Buck saved his master again. Summer had come. The ice on the river had melted. John was taking a boat down the river with two friends, Hans and Pete.

The river was wild and fast-moving. John was in the boat, using a long pole to move it through the water. Hans and Pete were on the bank, holding on to a long rope tied to the craft, in order to keep it steady. Buck was standing with them. As usual his eyes were on John.

The boat was getting near a very rough patch of water. There were many rocks poking out of the white foam. The boat began to be carried along quickly.

The two men on the bank did not know what to do. Hans wound his end of the rope round a tree. This made the craft come to a sudden halt. It turned right over and sent John flying into the water.

The helpless miner was in a wild stretch of the river in which not even a swimmer could live. Buck sprang into the water and swam straight towards his master. He fought his way through the foam until he reached John's side.

The miner reached out and held on to the dog's tail. Buck turned and tried to drag the man back to the shore.

He could not do it. The force of the rushing water was too strong. John and Buck found that they were being dragged down the river towards a number of great sharp rocks sticking out of the water like black teeth.

John knew that he could not reach the river bank. He scraped over one rock, crashed into a second and then held on to a third. He let go of the dog's tail.

"Go, Buck, go!" he shouted.

Buck was swept on down-stream. He heard his master's shout and raised his head out of the water. He could see the shore and he could hear Hans and Pete calling him.

Without the weight of his master clinging to his tail the dog was able to swim back towards the river bank. It was hard work, but in the end he got close to land. Hans and Pete were able to drag him on to the bank.

Both men knew that John would not be able to hold on to the rock for long. As fast as they could they tied one end of a piece of rope about Buck's body, holding on to the other end.

"Go back to John," cried Pete. "Swim, Buck, swim!"

Again the dog pushed out into the wild foam. This time he was swept past his master and on down the river by the power of the water.

On the bank Hans and Pete pulled on the rope and dragged Buck back to the land. The dog had hurt his ribs against a rock and had swallowed much water. The two men pumped the water out of him and Buck jumped back into the river.

This time he heard his master call out faintly above the roar of the water. He knew that John must be very weak.

Buck swam with all his might, taking the rope with him. This time he held on until he was in a straight line above John. Then he turned and let the force of the water sweep him down-river.

He went through the hissing foam with the speed of a train. He hit John with great force. The man let go of the rock and clung to Buck and the rope.

On the shore Hans and Pete started to tug on their end of the rope. Buck and John were pulled under the water and dragged towards the shore. Dog and man crashed against rocks and scraped along the bottom of the river, holding on to each other. After what seemed an age they reached the bank and were dragged on to dry land.

When John came round he stood up and limped over to Buck. The dog was lying on the ground, his eyes shut. Gently John felt him all over. He found three broken ribs.

"Right," said John. "We camp here."

And camp they did, until Buck's ribs healed and he was able to travel again.

A ROUGH RIDE

from "Lorna Doone" – by R.D. Blackmore

When I was about fifteen, I was big and strong for my age. Working all hours on our Exmoor farm in the West of England had made me that way. I also thought too much of myself. However, a meeting with a horse was to bring me down to earth in more ways than one.

One dark and wet November evening, my younger sister Annie and I went out into the farmyard to see what was making our ducks so noisy.

It had been pouring down with rain for a week past. The river which flowed close to our house had risen over its banks and was in full flood.

The ducks were scattered all along the rushing water's edge. They were staring out at the swollen water and quacking like mad things.

There in the middle of the water was a tree. Caught up against this tree was a gate which had been torn from its hinges and carried away. Clinging to the top of this gate and in danger at any moment of being swept off and drowned was our old drake, the father of most of the ducks on the farm.

Annie screamed at the sight of our beloved old bird in such danger. I liked not the look of it but I began to wade into the fierce current.

A man on the back of a horse came suddenly round the corner of the great ash-hedge on the other side of the stream.

"Ho, there!" he cried, "get thee back boy. The flood will carry thee down like a straw. I will do it for thee."

With that he spoke softly to his mare. She was young and proud and the colour of a strawberry. She arched up her neck, as if disliking the job but trusting her rider.

With dainty steps she entered the water. The rider gripped her sides with his knees, urging her on. She stopped and looked back, wondering. Then she went on until the water rushed over her shoulders.

The mare tossed up her lip, as if scorning the danger. Then the rush of the water swept her away and down the stream, past the gate. As they struggled through the water the man leaned forward in his saddle. He plucked the drake from the gate and carried him away.

In a moment all three were carried down-stream. The rider, still holding on to the drake, lay flat in his saddle and made for a bend of smooth water.

They landed some way away in our kitchen garden, where the winter cabbage was. Annie and I crept through the hedge to thank the rescuers. The man would not answer us until he had spoken to his mount.

"Sweetheart," he said gently, "I know you could have jumped across, but I had a good reason for making you swim. Well done, my Winnie."

Some way from us the drake clapped his wings, shook the water from his body and waddled off to his admiring family. The rider dismounted and looked at us.

He was short but strongly-built, fresh and ruddy-looking, with a short nose and keen blue eyes. He had a merry way with him. Yet he had a sharp, stern air, like the crack of a pistol if he did not like something.

"Well, young 'uns, what are you gaping at?" he asked.

"Your mare, sir," I said bravely. "I never saw such a horse. Will you let me ride her?"

"You could never ride her, lad. Winnie will carry no one but me. She would throw you off and kill you."

"Ride her?" I said with scorn. "I can ride any horse on Exmoor. Only I never use a saddle. Take it off."

The man looked at me and grinned. "The ground is soft enough for you to fall on," he said after a while. "Come out of this garden though, for the sake of the cabbages. By the way, I am your mother's cousin. Tom Faggus is my name, as everybody knows. And this is my young mare, Winnie."

What a fool I had been not to have known at once! Tom Faggus was the great highwayman. He was the most famous robber in these parts, and was famed for many daring hold-ups and escapes.

His mare Winnie was almost as well-known as her master. I had been a fool to offer to ride her, but I could not back down now for the sake of my pride.

Mr Faggus gave his mare a wink and she walked after him until we reached the open field.

"Are you sure, boy?" he asked me.

"Can she jump, sir?" I asked. "There is a good take-off on this side of the stream."

Mr Faggus laughed quietly. "A good fall-off, you mean. Well, there can be no great harm in it for you. We are a family of thick skulls."

"Let me get up," I said angrily.

Tom Faggus looked hard at me. Then he began to remove the saddle. Men from the farm were beginning to run up to see what was going on.

Tom spoke softly to the mare. "Not too hard, my dear," he told her. "Let him down gently into the wind and mud. That will be enough."

He took off the saddle. I leapt on to Winnie's back. I pushed the mare into a walk and then a trot. She moved easily, as if pleased to find such a light weight upon her back. In my ignorance I thought she knew that I could ride a little, and was afraid of me.

"Gee-up," I cried, showing off in front of the others. "Show what you are made of," and I dug my heels into her sides.

Tom Faggus whistled. The horse took off like a great spring uncoiled. I felt her hind legs coming up under her and I knew that I was in for it.

First she reared upright in the air. In doing so she struck me full on the nose with her neck, bringing my blood flowing. Then she stuck her fore feet in the mud and kicked her hind ones to the heavens. Finding me still sticking to her like wax, away she flew with me.

I was being carried faster than I had ever ridden before. Winnie drove straight at a stone wall.

"Jump off, John!" screamed my sister.

At the last moment the mare turned with the speed of light. We were so close to the wall that my knee brushed against it.

"Mux me!" I cried, for my breeches were broken, and short words went the furthest, "if you kill me, you shall die with me!"

Then Winnie took the courtyard gate at a leap, knocking my words between my teeth. She went over a hedge and headed for the water-meadows. I lay on her neck and wished I had never been born.

We seemed to be faster than the wind and to scatter the clouds as we went. All I knew of the speed we made was the flash of the mare's shoulders, and her mane like trees in a tempest. I felt the earth under us rushing away, and the air left far behind us. My breath came and went. I prayed to God, and was sorry to be so late doing so.

All the long swift while I clung to Winnie's shoulders. I dug in my finger-nails and toes. I was proud of holding on so long, though sure of being beaten.

In a fury at feeling me on her still, she jumped across the wide water-trough sideways, to and fro, until no breath was left in me.

Branches from the trees whipped across my face, and thorns from the bushes scratched my hands and arms. I longed to give up and die quietly on the ground.

Suddenly there came a shrill whistle from close to the house. The mare stopped, as if shot. Then she set off for home with the speed of a swallow, and going as smoothly and silently. I had never dreamt of such gentle movement.

I sat up again, but my strength was all spent, and no time left to recover it. At last, as the mare rose at our gate like a bird, I fell off into the mud.

"Well done, lad," said Mr Faggus, as they all gathered round me. "Not at all bad work, my boy. I did not think you would stick on so long."

"I should have stuck on much longer sir, if her sides had not been wet. She was so slippery."

"Boy, you are right. She has given many the slip," said the highwayman with a laugh. "Vex not because I laugh, John. Winnie is like a sweetheart to me, and better than any of them be. None but I can ride my Winnie mare."

ELEPHANT HUNT

from "Trader Horn" – by Trader Horn

The elephant is a mighty beast. As a rule he does harm to no one. But from time to time one is driven away from the herd by the others. This rogue elephant may then become a danger to all men. I was to find this out for myself.

I had been a trader on the Ivory Coast of Africa for many years, but the beauty of the land always amazed me.

On this trip I had been visiting the villages along the banks of a great lake. I sailed my large canoe from place to place. It was piled high with such trade goods as bags of salt, knives, plates, files, guns and gunpowder. These I would exchange for carved canoe paddles, elephant tusks and any other goods the people had to offer.

The water of the lake around the canoe was as clear as dew. I spent hours staring over the side at all the wonders beneath the surface. I marvelled at the fish, the coloured rocks, and the weeds that waved in the water and shone as if the sun was pouring colour into them.

After a number of days I left the lake. The twenty men I had hired paddled our canoe up a wide and winding river.

On either side great trees grew down to the water's edge. Gay parrots, butterflies and dragon-flies swooped in and out of the trees and skimmed across the water in front of us. As we passed the sandbanks lining the shore huge crocodiles slipped into the water and eased their lazy way across the river. Tick-birds perched on the heads of these great creatures and picked their teeth free from insects. Hippos wallowed in the mud on either side of our craft.

That night we slept on a sandbank. I always chose such a place to rest because cool breezes would blow over them. But the night was not a quiet one. For hour after hour I could hear animals coming down to the water to drink. I could hear the growl of the tree-leopards, the chatter of monkeys, and from time to time the unusual sound of the great gorillas beating their chests with their fists as if they were drums.

Early the next morning we set out again. Ahead of us lay an island in the middle of the river. White-winged sea-birds who had made the long journey inland from the Atlantic to lay their eggs, fluttered about us as we paddled.

Waiting just off the shore of the island was a large war canoe. A dozen warriors came out in the canoe to greet us. Seated in the prow was an old chief I knew well. He hardly spared the time to greet me before he was talking quickly.

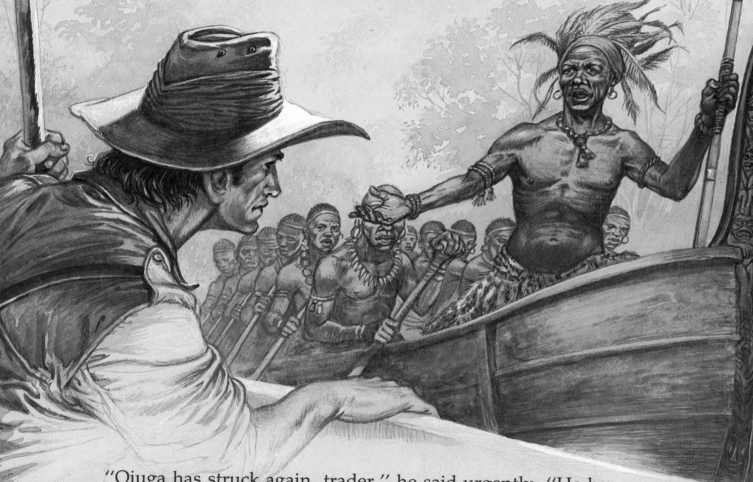

"Ojuga has struck again, trader," he said urgently. "He has killed two children from my village. He cannot be far away. You have the most powerful rifle in this part of the country. Will you go after him? You are our best chance."

I nodded. Ojuga was a great killer elephant, famed throughout the area. Years ago he had been cast out of his herd because he was so fierce and bad-tempered. He had become a lonely night prowler. Over the years he had killed many men and women from local villages. The name Ojuga meant Hunger.

"I'll do my best," I told the chief. "Which way did he go?"

The old man pointed up-river. "That way," he said. "He left the village about an hour ago. Take care, trader."

For several hours my helpers paddled the canoe past the trees crowding down to the river bank. I held on to my Snyder rifle. I had three of them in the canoe. The other men had their spears, the long sharp weapons known as *assegais*.

After a time we turned into a narrow stream leading off the main river. We slowed down and looked from side to side. We seemed to sense that the beast we were hunting was not far away.

We rounded a bend and saw something that made me tighten my hold on my rifle.

On the left-hand side of the stream, walking slowly along the bank, was a huge bull elephant. He was the biggest of his sort I had ever seen. His skin hung loose about his sides and legs, looking like mud-coloured overalls. His great nodding head held two large tusks jutting out ahead of him.

He entered the water some way in front of us. Filling his trunk with water he sprayed it all over himself. We had a fine view of him.

I could have shot him and perhaps killed him while he was crossing the river, but the great beast always held his head in such a way as to make it hard to shoot him through the eye, one certain way of killing him.

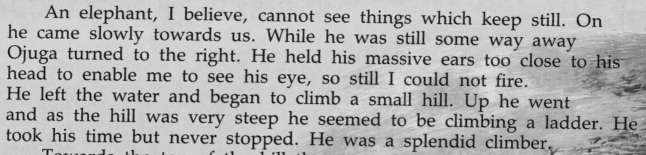

An elephant, I believe, cannot see things which keep still. On he came slowly towards us. While he was still some way away Ojuga turned to the right. He held his massive ears too close to his head to enable me to see his eye, so still I could not fire. He left the water and began to climb a small hill. Up he went and as the hill was very steep he seemed to be climbing a ladder. He took his time but never stopped. He was a splendid climber.

Towards the top of the hill the elephant suddenly made a great noise, something like a trumpet being played loudly and out of tune. The path here was narrow and the great beast wanted to make sure that he had a clear path ahead.

Then, for no apparent reason, Ojuga stopped and half-turned. This was my chance. I fired. No result. I fired again, with a rifle handed to me by one of the men in the canoe. Another shot behind the ear, no result. The elephant began to lumber away.

I jumped out of the canoe on to a sandbank and aimed my rifle again. Before I could press the trigger the great beast suddenly fell backwards. The shots had taken effect.

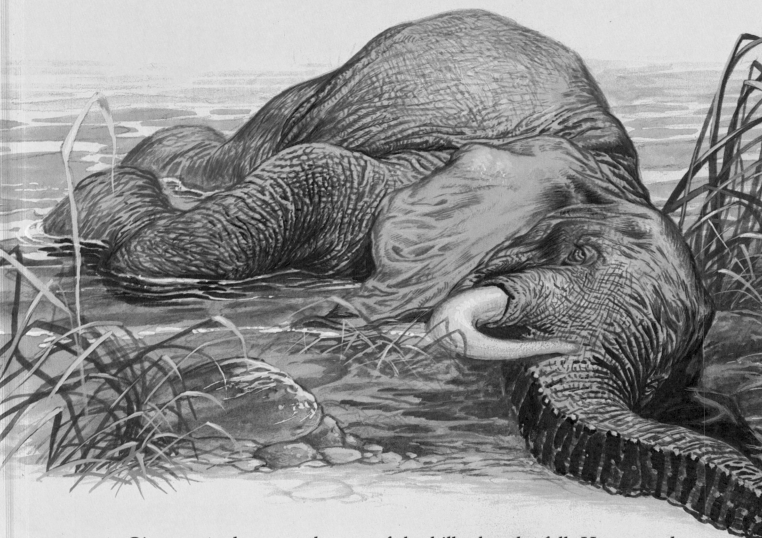

Ojuga was almost at the top of the hill when he fell. He seemed to bring most of the hill down with him. Down, down he came, amid a shower of loosened rock and a cloud of dust. He fell into the stream, just ahead of the canoe, with his head on the sandbank and his huge body in the water.

I ran along the sandbank. The elephant was quite dead. The hind part of his body was covered with a pile of rock and dust.

I sent two of my men to fetch the chief. He must have been following close behind, because it was not long before the war canoes came into view.

The old man stepped out on to the sandbank. He shook my hand and thanked me.

"You were lucky, trader," he added.

"How so?" I asked.

"I have known Ojuga since I was a boy," the old chief said slowly. "He was hunted by my father and my grandfather before him. Once, when I was a young man, I even managed to throw a spear into his side, but he went away and healed himself. One day he returned and charged at me while I was picking bananas. Two of my men shot him at close range, but Ojuga turned and trampled them to death. He has lived long and done much harm. But now he lies here, the greatest of all elephants."

Fires were lit and the men and women danced. They made up a new song. I am told that it is still sung to this day. The song went: "Ojuga was mighty and feared. He slew many men, but now he is slain and eaten."

As the dancing and singing went on through the night, I found that I was becoming sad. I thought about the beast I had shot. He had been a noble sight in his life.

I wondered what Ojuga could have thought about being cast out of his tribe and forced to wander by himself for year after year. He must have had a lonely time of it.

Perhaps in a way I had helped him by shooting him on that hill. He had been growing old. Sooner or later he would have gone down to drink in the swamp and would have found that he could not pull his great weight out of it.

The death that I had given him had been grander than that. There had been majesty in his great fall from the hill.

MONTMORENCY

by Jerome K. Jerome

There were four of us – George, and William Samuel Harris, and myself, and Montmorency the dog. We decided that we should have fresh air, exercise and quiet by taking a boat up the river Thames.

Everyone was keen on the idea, except Montmorency. He never did care for the river, did Montmorency.

"It's all very well for you fellows," he seemed to complain, "you like it, but *I* don't. There's nothing for me to do. Scenery is not in my line, and I don't smoke. If I see a rat, you won't stop; and if I go to sleep, you start fooling about with the boat, and slop me overboard. If you ask me, I call the whole thing stupid."

We were three to one, however, and the matter was agreed. We decided that we would sleep out on fine nights and hotel it, and inn it and pub it when it was wet, or we felt like a change.

Montmorency was greatly in favour of this. He likes company. Give him something noisy and not very nice and he is happy. To look at Montmorency you would imagine that he was an angel sent upon the earth, for some reason unknown to mankind, in the shape of a small fox-terrier. There is a sort of Oh-what-a-wicked-world-this-is-and-how-I-wish-I-could-do-something-to-make-it-better-and-nobler expression about Montmorency that has been known to bring tears to the eyes of old ladies and gentlemen.

When he first came to live with me, I never thought I should be able to get him to stop long. I used to sit down and look at him, as he sat on the rug and looked up at me, and think: "Oh, that dog will never live. He will be snatched up to the bright skies in a chariot, that is what will happen to him."

But, when I had paid for about a dozen chickens that he had killed; and had dragged him, growling and kicking, by the scruff of his neck, out of a hundred and fourteen street fights; and I had had a dead cat brought round for my inspection by an angry female, who called me a murderer; and had been taken to court by the man next-door-but-one for having a wild dog at large, that had kept him pinned up in his own tool-shed, afraid to come out for over two hours on a cold night; and had learned that the gardener, unknown to myself, had won quite a lot of money by backing the dog to kill rats in a certain length of time, then I began to think that maybe they'd let him remain on earth for a bit longer, after all.

To hang about a stable, and collect a gang of the scruffiest dogs to be found in the town, and to lead them out to march round the slums to fight other scruffy dogs, is Montmorency's idea of "life", and so he was quite keen on the idea of stopping at pubs with stables on our river holiday.

The wretched dog made his presence felt as soon as the three of us started packing for our holiday. He was in it all, of course. Montmorency's ambition in life is to get in the way and be sworn at. If he can squirm in anywhere where he is particularly not wanted, and be a perfect nuisance, and make people mad, and have things thrown at his head, then he feels that his day has not been wasted.

To get somebody to stumble over him, and curse him steadily for an hour, is his highest aim and object; and, when he has succeeded in this, his conceit becomes quite unbearable.

He came and sat down on things, just when they were wanted to be packed; and he had the idea that whenever Harris or George reached out their hands for anything, it was his cold damp nose they wanted. He put his leg into the jam, and he worried the teaspoons, and he pretended that the lemons were rats, and got into the hamper and killed three of them before Harris could hit him with the frying pan.

Harris said I encouraged him. I didn't encourage him. A dog like that doesn't want any encouragement. It's the natural sin that is born in him that makes him do things like that.

When we actually got going on the holiday Montmorency was no better. He let us down very badly on the first day. We had moored the boat at Marlow and decided to go for a walk along the High Street there. Coming along the road we met a cat.

When Montmorency meets a cat, the whole street knows about it; and there is enough bad language wasted in ten seconds to last an ordinary respectable man all his life, with care.

Half-way along the High Street a cat darted out from one of the houses in front of us, and began to trot across the road. Montmorency gave a cry of joy and flew after his prey.

His victim was a large black tom. I never saw a larger cat, nor a tougher-looking one. It had lost half its tail, one of its ears, and a large portion of its nose. It was a long, strong-looking animal. It had a calm, contented look about it.

Montmorency went for that poor cat at a tremendous speed; but the cat did not hurry up—it did not seem to have grasped the idea that its life was in danger. It trotted quietly on until the terrier was almost upon it, and then it turned round and sat in the middle of the road, and looked at Montmorency with a gentle, inquiring expression that said:

"Yes! You want me?"

Montmorency does not lack courage; but there was something about the look of that cat that might have chilled the heart of the boldest dog. He stopped abruptly, and looked at the tom.

Neither spoke, but the conversation that one could imagine was clearly as follows:

THE CAT: "Can I do anything for you?"

MONTMORENCY: "No—no, thanks."

THE CAT: "Don't mind speaking, if you really want anything, you know."

MONTMORENCY: (*backing down the High Street*): "Oh no—not at all—certainly—don't you trouble. I—I am afraid I've made a mistake. I thought I knew you. Sorry I disturbed you."

THE CAT: "Not at all—quite a pleasure. Sure you don't want anything, now?"

MONTMORENCY: (*still backing*): "Not at all, thanks—not at all—very kind of you. Good morning."

THE CAT: "Good morning."

43

Then the cat rose, and continued his trot; and Montmorency, fitting what he calls his tail carefully into its groove, came back to us, and took up an unimportant position in the rear.

To this day, if you say the word "Cats!" to Montmorency, he will visibly shrink and look up piteously at you, as if to say: "Please don't."

Neither was the dog a great help when it came to helping with the cooking. One evening George offered to cook us a magnificent stew on the banks of the river. It seemed a great idea. George gathered wood and lit a fire, and we threw plenty of potatoes into the pot, and half a pork pie, and a few cracked eggs, and a bit of cold boiled bacon, and half a tin of potted salmon.

I forget what else we added, but I know nothing was wasted. Towards the end, Montmorency, who had shown great interest in the proceedings throughout, strolled away with an earnest and thoughtful air. He reappeared a few minutes afterwards, with a dead water-rat in his mouth, which he evidently wished to present as his contribution to the dinner; whether in a sarcastic spirit, or with a general desire to assist, I cannot say.

It was a great success, that Irish stew. We finished up with tea and cherry tart. Montmorency had a fight with the kettle during tea-time, and came off a poor second.

Throughout the trip he had seemed puzzled by the kettle. He would sit and watch it as it boiled, with a blank expression. He would try to rouse it every now and then by growling at it. When it began to splutter and steam he regarded it as a challenge, and would want to fight it, only, at that precise moment, someone would always dash up and bear the kettle away before he could get at it.

Today he made up his mind to succeed. At the first sound the kettle made, he rose, growling, and advanced towards it. It was only a little kettle, but it was full of courage, and it up and spat at him.

"Ah! would you!" growled Montmorency, showing his teeth; "I'll teach you to cheek a hard-working, respectable dog; you miserable, long-nosed, dirty-looking scoundrel, you. Come on!"

And he rushed at that poor little kettle, and seized it by the spout.

Then, across the evening stillness, broke a blood-curdling yelp, and Montmorency left the boat, and ran three times round the island, stopping every now and then to bury his nose in a bit of cool mud.

From that day Montmorency regarded the kettle with a mixture of awe, suspicion and hate. Whenever he saw it, he would growl and back at a rapid rate, with his tail shut down, and the moment it was put up on the stove he would promptly climb out of the boat, and sit on the bank, till the whole tea business was over.

George got out his banjo after supper, and wanted to play it. He met with little success. Harris's language was enough to put any man off; added to which, Montmorency sat and howled steadily, right through the performance. It was not giving a man a fair chance.

"What does he want to howl like that for when I'm playing?" George exclaimed indignantly, while taking aim at the dog with a boot.

"What do you want to play like that for when he is howling?" Harris retorted, catching the boot. "You let him alone. He can't help howling. He's got a musical ear, and your playing *makes* him howl."

So George gave up the study of the banjo until he got home.

Of all the towns we visited as we sailed up the Thames, Montmorency preferred Oxford. We spent two very pleasant days there. There are plenty of dogs in the town of Oxford. Montmorency had eleven fights on the first day, and fourteen on the second, and evidently thought that he had gone to heaven.

Even when Montmorency was quiet I did not altogether trust him. He is a fox-terrier, and fox-terriers are born with about four times as much sin in them as other dogs.

I remember being in the lobby of the Haymarket Stores one day, and all round about me were dogs, waiting for the return of their owners who were shopping inside. There was a mastiff, and one or two collies, and a St Bernard, a few retrievers and Newfoundlands, a boar-hound, a French poodle, with plenty of hair round its head, but mangy in the middle; a bulldog, and a couple of Yorkshire tykes.

There they sat, patient, good, and thoughtful. Peace seemed to reign in the lobby. Then a sweet young lady entered, leading a meek-looking fox-terrier, and left him, chained up there, between the bulldog and the poodle. He sat and looked about him for a minute. Then he cast his eyes up to the ceiling, and seemed, judging from his expression, to be thinking of his mother. Then he yawned. Then he looked round at the other dogs, all silent; grave and good.

He looked at the bulldog, sleeping dreamlessly on his right. He looked at the poodle, straight and proud, on his left. Then, without a word of warning, he bit the poodle on the leg. A yelp of agony rang through the quiet shades of the lobby.

The fox-terrier obviously then decided to make things lively all round. He sprang over the poodle and attacked a collie, and the collie woke up and at once started a noisy battle with the poodle. The fox-terrier came back to his own place, and caught the bulldog by his ear, and tried to throw him away. The bulldog went for everything he could reach, including the hall-porter. This gave the dear little fox-terrier the chance to enjoy a fight of his own with an equally willing Yorkshire tyke.

By this time all the other dogs in the place were fighting as if their lives depended upon it.

47

The whole lobby seemed upside down, and the din was terrific. A crowd gathered outside the store, asking who was being murdered, and why? Men came with poles and ropes, and tried to separate the dogs, and the police were sent for.

In the midst of the riot that sweet young lady returned, and snatched up that sweet little dog of hers (he had laid the tyke up for a month, and had on the expression, now, of a new-born lamb) into her arms, and kissed him, and asked if he was killed, and what those great nasty brutes of dogs had been doing to him; and he gazed up into her face with a look that seemed to say: "Oh, I'm so glad you've come to take me away from this disgraceful scene!"

She said that the people at the store had no right to allow great savage things like those other dogs to be put with respectable people's dogs, and that she had a great mind to report them to somebody.

Such is the nature of fox-terriers, and, therefore, knowing him as I do, I always regard Montmorency with great caution. However, I must admit that on that trip there was one occasion when the sound of his bark was the sweetest noise I had ever heard.

It happened one night. We had moored the boat among many others among a group of islands in the river. George and I left Harris and Montmorency on board and went ashore to walk round Henley. We agreed that when we returned, we would shout from the shore and that Harris would row ashore in the small boat and collect us.

"Don't go asleep, old man," we warned him as we left.

The town of Henley was full of bustle that night. We met a fair number of people we knew about the town, and in their pleasant company the time slipped by somewhat quickly. It was nearly eleven o'clock before we left to walk back to our boat.

It was a dismal night, coldish, with a thin rain falling; and as we trudged through the dark, silent fields, talking low to each other, and wondering if we were going in the right direction, we thought of the cosy boat, with the bright light streaming through the tight-drawn canvas; of Harris and Montmorency waiting for us, and wished that we were there.

We struck the tow-path running along the river bank at length. We passed Shiplake as the clock was striking the quarter to twelve; and then George said thoughtfully:

"You don't happen to remember which of the islands it was, do you?"

"No," I replied, beginning to grow thoughtful too. "I don't. How many are there?"

"Only four," answered George. "It will be all right, if Harris is awake."

"And if not?" I asked, but we dismissed that thought.

We shouted when we came opposite the first island, but there was no reply; so we went on to the second and tried there, and got the same result.

"Oh! I remember now," said George, "it was the third one."

And we ran on hopefully to the third island, and shouted.

No answer!

The case was becoming serious. It was now past midnight. The hotels at Henley would be crammed; and we could not go round, knocking at doors in the middle of the night, asking for a bed.

In despair we tried the fourth island, but met with no better success. The rain was coming down fast now. We were wet to the skin, and cold and miserable. We began to wonder whether there were four islands or more, or whether, in the dark, we were even near any islands.

Just as we had given up all hope, I thought I caught sight of a flicker of a light out on the water. I shouted loudly and waited. Then, to our joy, we heard the answering bark of Montmorency. The dog barked loud and long enough to wake up Harris, for in about five minutes we saw the lighted rowing boat coming towards us in the dark, and heard Harris's sleepy voice asking where we were.

Slowly he took us back to our boat. Oh, how delightful it was to be safe on board after all our trials and fears. We ate a hearty supper, George and I, and for the first time in ages we looked approvingly at Montmorency!

THE WAR HORSE

from "Black Beauty" – by Anna Sewell

Sometimes in my dreams I hear the noise of battle again. The cannons roar in my ears. The shouts of the dead and dying echo through the night.

Captain is my name. I am a war-horse. It is my job to carry my master into battle.

When I was still a very young horse I was chosen by an army officer for this task. The year was about 1853. My officer served in the cavalry. Cavalry soldiers charge at the enemy on horseback, their swords in their hands.

After it was decided that I had the makings of a war-horse I had to be trained for the job. At first I found this very pleasant. There were many horses all together. We were well fed and well looked after.

We did our training in a large field next to an army camp. There were at least fifty of us. Every morning we turned out, looking very smart, with our masters on our backs.

For weeks we were trained to trot together in straight lines. At the word of command we would turn to the left or to the right. If a trumpet sounded over the field we would all dash forwards at great speed. I found this part very exciting.

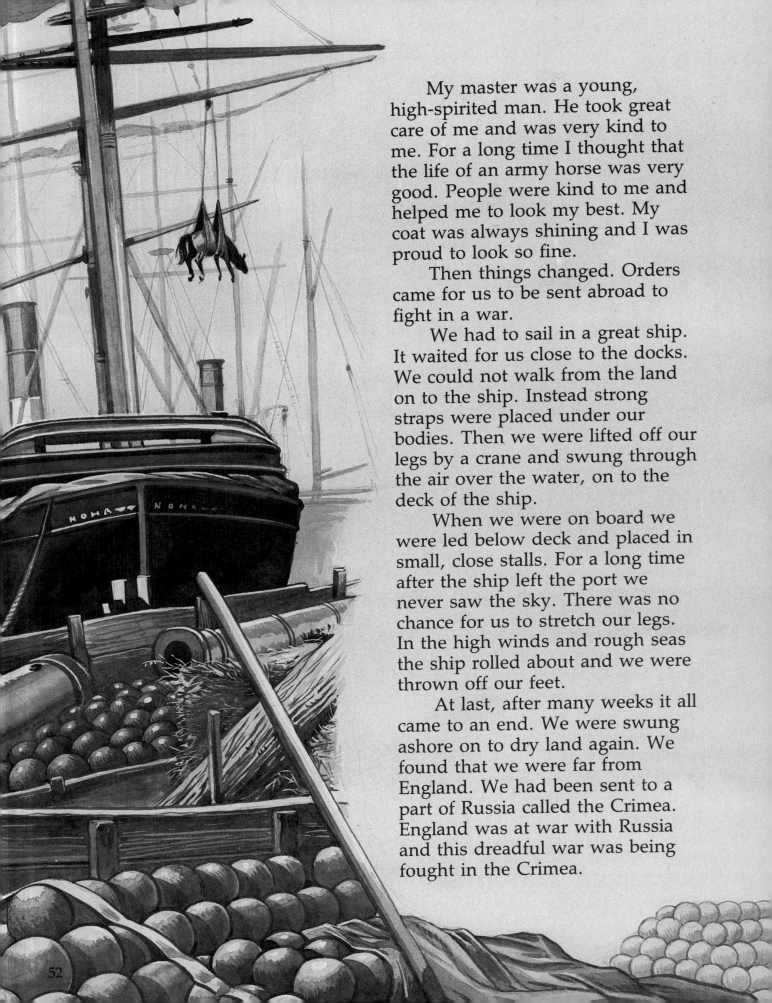

My master was a young, high-spirited man. He took great care of me and was very kind to me. For a long time I thought that the life of an army horse was very good. People were kind to me and helped me to look my best. My coat was always shining and I was proud to look so fine.

Then things changed. Orders came for us to be sent abroad to fight in a war.

We had to sail in a great ship. It waited for us close to the docks. We could not walk from the land on to the ship. Instead strong straps were placed under our bodies. Then we were lifted off our legs by a crane and swung through the air over the water, on to the deck of the ship.

When we were on board we were led below deck and placed in small, close stalls. For a long time after the ship left the port we never saw the sky. There was no chance for us to stretch our legs. In the high winds and rough seas the ship rolled about and we were thrown off our feet.

At last, after many weeks it all came to an end. We were swung ashore on to dry land again. We found that we were far from England. We had been sent to a part of Russia called the Crimea. England was at war with Russia and this dreadful war was being fought in the Crimea.

The land in which we had arrived was very different to England. Life was hard there. We lived in great camps which held many tents. Our masters did their best to look after us. Most of them were very fond of their horses. They did everything that they could to help us, in spite of the cold, the rain and the snow.

It was not long before we were sent into battle. We took part in a number of engagements. Sometimes we had to stand waiting for hours before the order to move was given. But then the trumpet would sound and we would advance. That was the part I always liked best.

When the order to charge was given we would leap forward at a great rate. We paid no heed to the cannon balls, bullets and bayonets that awaited us at the end of the charge. As long as we felt our rider firm and safe in the saddle, and his hand steady on the reins, not one of us was afraid.

My noble master and I were in many actions together without a wound. Around me I saw horses shot down with bullets, cut with lances, and gashed by swords. I never feared for myself. My master's cheery voice made me feel as if he and I could not be killed.

I saw many brave men cut down. I heard the cries and groans of the dying. I cantered over ground slippery with blood. But I never felt terror – until one dreadful day I shall never forget.

One autumn morning we turned out an hour before dawn, ready for work. The men stood by their horses, waiting for orders. The light grew brighter and in the distance we could hear the sound of guns.

One of the officers rode up and gave the order to mount. In a second every man was in his saddle. Every horse stood waiting. My dear master and I were at the head of the line.

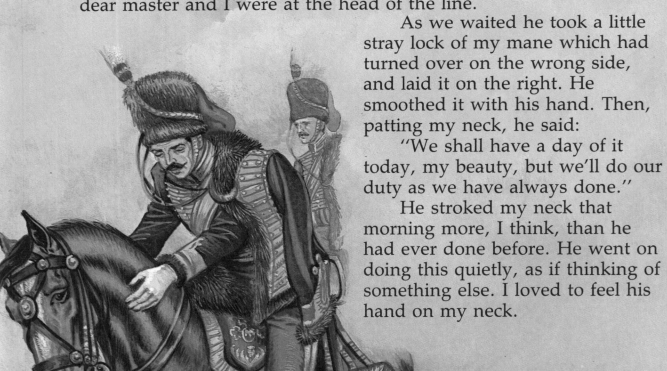

As we waited he took a little stray lock of my mane which had turned over on the wrong side, and laid it on the right. He smoothed it with his hand. Then, patting my neck, he said:

"We shall have a day of it today, my beauty, but we'll do our duty as we have always done."

He stroked my neck that morning more, I think, than he had ever done before. He went on doing this quietly, as if thinking of something else. I loved to feel his hand on my neck.

I cannot tell all that happened that day, but I will tell of the last charge we made. We rode across a valley right in front of the enemy's guns. By this time we were well used to their roar, the rattle of musket fire, and the flying of shot near us. But never had I been under such fire as we rode through on that day.

From the right, from the left, and from the front, shot and shell poured in on us. Many a brave man went down. Many a horse fell, flinging his rider to the earth. Many a horse without a rider ran wildly out of the ranks.

Fearful as it was, no one stopped, no one turned back. Every moment the ranks of the riders were thinned. As our comrades fell we closed in closer together. We drew closer to the cannon, all clouded in white smoke, with the red fire flashing through it. Our pace became faster and faster.

My master, my dear master, was cheering on his comrades with his right arm raised on high. One of the great iron balls struck him. I felt him stagger with the shock, though he made no sound. I tried to check my speed, but the sword dropped from his right hand, the rein fell from his left, and he fell to the earth.

The other riders swept past us. By the force of their charge I was driven from the spot where he fell.

I wanted to keep my place by his side, and not leave him under the rush of horses' feet, but it was in vain. Now, without a master or friend, I was alone on that great killing ground. Fear took me as it had never taken me before.

I trembled and tried to join the ranks of the horses still with riders. Men beat me off with the flats of their swords, in case I got in their way and brought them down.

Just then, a soldier whose horse had been killed under him, caught at my bridle and mounted me. With this new master I again went forward. But our brave company could go no further. The ground was thick with bodies. Still the guns fired. Those who remained alive after the fierce battle for guns, came riding back over the same ground.

Some of the horses were so badly wounded that they could hardly move for loss of blood. Others were trying to drag themselves along on three legs. A few tried to drag themselves to their feet. Their groans were awful to hear. The battle was over.

Afterwards soldiers went out with guns to shoot the badly wounded horses. The ones which were not so badly hurt were brought back and helped. In our stables only one in four were left alive.

I never saw my dear master again. I believe he fell dead from the saddle. I never loved another master so well. I went into other battles, but was only once wounded. When the war was over I returned to England, as sound and strong as when I went out.

Sometimes I wonder what the war was all about. Why did my fine young master have to die? But it is all too much for me. To tell the truth, I can think of no reason for it at all.

COYOTE, OR THE PRAIRIE WOLF

by Francis Bret Harte

Blown out of the prairie in twilight and dew,
Half bold and half timid, yet lazy all through;
Loth ever to leave, and yet fearful to stay,
He limps in the clearing, – an outcast in grey.

A shade on the stubble, a ghost by the wall,
Now leaping, now limping, now risking a fall,
Lop-eared and large-jointed, but ever alway
A thoroughly vagabond outcast in grey.

Here, Carlo, old fellow, he's one of your kind, –
Go seek him, and bring him in out of the wind.
What! snarling, my Carlo! So – even dogs may
Deny their own kin in the outcast in grey!

Well, take what you will, – though it be on the sly,
Marauding or begging, – I shall not ask why;
But will call it a dole, just to help on his way
A four-footed friar in orders of grey!

THE PICK OF THE PUPPIES

from "Jock of the Bushveld"
by Sir Percy Fitzpatrick

I needed a dog. My job in South Africa many years ago was to bring food and supplies up to the gold mining camps in waggons, drawn by teams of oxen. A number of waggons would travel together in this way on long, hard journeys for many days at a time, resting at night.

I felt that a good dog would serve both as a friend and as a guard. Finding one, however, was no easy task.

One day, old Jess, a bull-terrier belonging to Ted, one of the other transport riders, gave birth to six puppies. Ted said that he was willing to get rid of them.

The puppies were kept with their mother in a nest in one of the waggons. Five of the pups were fat, strong, yellow little chaps with dark muzzles. The sixth was different. He was a poor little rat of a thing, about half the size of the others. He was not yellow like them, but a sort of dirty pale half-and-half colour with some dark, faint wavy lines all over him.

Most of the fellows said it would be a good thing to drown the odd one because he spoiled the litter. But in the end he was allowed to live.

I offered to take him rather than let him be drowned. All the other puppies had already been claimed by drivers who knew Ted better than I did. Ted agreed that I might take the puppy when he was ready to leave his mother.

As they grew older and were able to crawl about, the pups were taken off the waggons when we camped for the night and put on the ground. Jess would watch us quietly as we took them in our hands, to put them down or lift them back again.

I began to look after the sixth puppy. I felt sorry for him because he was small and weak. The other puppies used to push him away from his food and trample on him. When they were old enough to play they used to pull his ears and bully him. Many a time I had to rescue him and feed him on bread and milk.

I began to notice little things about him. I got to be quite fond of the little beggar. He was always cheerful and brave and it seemed that there might be some good stuff in him after all.

The other puppies would tumble over him and take his food from him. They would bump into him when he was stooping over the dish of milk and porridge. His head was so big and his legs so weak that he would tip up and go head over heels into the dish. We were always picking him out of the food and scraping it off him. Half the time he was wet and sticky, and the other half covered with porridge and sand, baked hard by the sun.

One day just after the waggons had started, I took a final look round to see if anything had been left behind. I found the little chap – who was still tiny – trying to walk through the long grass. He was not big enough or strong enough to push his way through. He stumbled and tripped at every step, but he got up again each time with his little tail standing straight up, his head erect, and his ears cocked.

He looked as proud and important as if he owned the whole world. How he fell out of the waggon no one knew. Perhaps the big puppies had pushed him out.

The other transport riders thought more of the sixth puppy when I caught up with them and told them of his brave efforts to walk through the long grass. But they continued to call him 'The Rat'. He really was very ugly, and as he grew older he got worse.

He was very silent, hardly ever barking. One day however he did make a noise. One of the oxen caught sight of the pup all alone and came up to sniff at him. 'The Rat' stood quite still with his stumpy tail cocked up and his head a little on one side. When the huge ox's nose was just in front of him he gave a funny, sharp little bark. It was as if he had exploded like a firecracker. The ox nearly fell over with fright and turned and trotted off.

'The Rat' was not a bit like other puppies. If anyone fired off a gun or cracked one of the big whips the whole five would yell at the top of their voices and would run away at once. The odd puppy would drop his bone with a start, or would jump round. His ears and tail would flicker up and down for a second. Then he would slowly bristle all over, and with his head cocked first on one side and then on the other, stare hard towards the noise. But he never ran away.

No matter how many of the other puppies attacked him, or how they bit or pulled him, he never once let out a yelp. With four or five on top of him you would see him on his back, snapping left and right with his bare white teeth.

Before long it was plain that most of the other puppies were leaving 'The Rat' alone. The reason was obvious. Instead of wasting his breath in making a noise, the odd puppy simply bit hard and hung on. No one could bully him, he fought back too hard.

The day came when Ted announced to the rest of us that the puppies were now ready to leave their mother. We could come along to his waggon and collect them.

As the drivers gathered before the waggon Ted came out.

"Bill can't take his pup," he told us.

Every man among us stepped forward. Bill's pup was the first pick, the best of the litter, the biggest and strongest of the lot. Several of the others said that they would take it. Ted shook his head.

"No," he said, "you had a good pick in the first place." Then he turned to me and said: "You only had the last choice. You can have Bill's pup if you like."

It seemed too good to be true. I could hardly wait to pick up the best pup. I went forward to claim him from the pile. As I did so the odd puppy came forward and licked my hand.

I had forgotten all about him. But the sight of him made me think of his odd ways, his bravery, and the fact that I was the only friend he had in the world. I knew what I must do.

"Ted," I said, waiting to hear the others laugh. "If you don't mind, I'll stick to 'The Rat'."

If I had fired off a gun the others could not have been more surprised. When they saw that I meant what I said, Ted spoke for all of them.

"Well, I'm hanged," he said.

"He's mine," I said firmly.

I took him in hand at once – for now he really belonged to me – and set about training the pup. Dogs are like people. What they learn when they are young they do not forget. I began early with 'The Rat', and tried to help him.

To start with I gave him a new name. From now on he was Jock, and that was how he was known to everyone.

Then I began to teach him obedience. The lesson began when he got his saucer of porridge in the morning. I put it in front of him and then tapped him on the nose each time he tried to dive into it.

At first he fought to get at it. Then he tried to back away and dodge round the other side. Then he became dazed, and thought it was not meant for him at all.

In a few days, however, I got him to lie still and take the food only when I patted him and pushed him towards it. In a very little time he got on so well that I could put his food down and he would not touch it until I told him to.

Jock would lie with his head on his paws and his nose right up against the saucer, so as to lose no time when the order came. But he would not touch it until the order came: ''Take it''.

His courage became well known among the miners and transport drivers. One day, while he was still a puppy, he finished his saucer of food under the rough camp table on which we put our food to keep it from the ants.

He had been standing close to the leg of the table. He stretched lazily and his hip came into contact with the table leg.

In an instant he changed completely. The hair on his back bristled. His head went up at one end and his tail at the other. He shook with rage. He thought that one of the other pups had come up on him from behind.

He was too proud to look round and appear nervous. He glared straight ahead and growled. He stood like that, not moving. Then he relaxed and stretched again.

The same thing happened again. His hip struck the table; he thought he was being stalked, and he growled with rage. One could not imagine so small a dog being in so great a temper.

Again, after a long time, he relaxed. Again his hip touched the table leg. This time it was all over in a second. Jock seemed to feel that three times was more than any dog could stand. He turned round with a great snarl – and bumped his nose against the table leg.

A great shout of laughter went up from all the men. Jock looked rather foolish. He gave us a feeble wag of his tail and waddled off as fast as he could.

Then Ted nodded over at me, and said: "I believe you have got the best after all!"

And I was too proud to speak.

65

THE CHASE

from "Moby Dick" – by Herman Melville

For years Captain Ahab had chased the great white whale, known as Moby Dick, from sea to sea. He swore that one day he would find the beast and destroy it.

Ahab hated the white whale with a great passion that filled his life. Once he had sailed his ship close to the monster, but Moby Dick had been too quick and too strong. He had turned on the whalers and put them to flight. In doing so he had delivered a terrible blow on Ahab, shattering his leg and causing him to lose it.

Somehow he got back to port, fitted out another vessel and gathered a crew to go in search of the white whale.

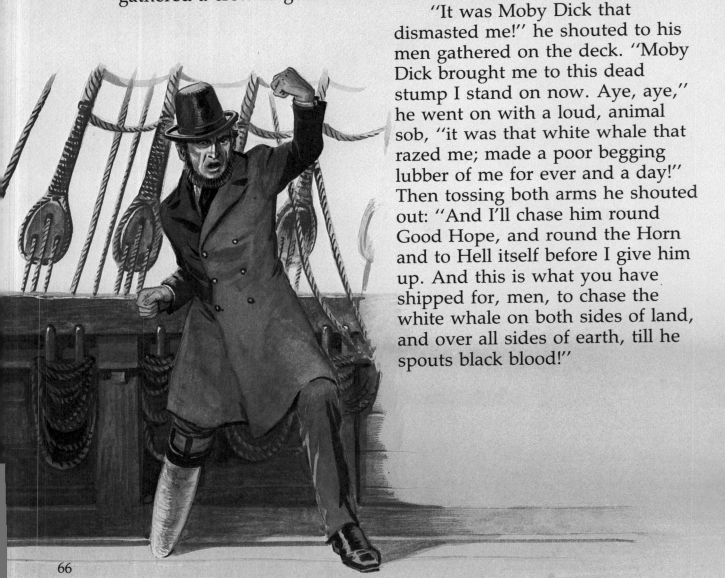

"It was Moby Dick that dismasted me!" he shouted to his men gathered on the deck. "Moby Dick brought me to this dead stump I stand on now. Aye, aye," he went on with a loud, animal sob, "it was that white whale that razed me; made a poor begging lubber of me for ever and a day!" Then tossing both arms he shouted out: "And I'll chase him round Good Hope, and round the Horn and to Hell itself before I give him up. And this is what you have shipped for, men, to chase the white whale on both sides of land, and over all sides of earth, till he spouts black blood!"

So the great voyage began. From sea to sea the whaling ship *Pequod* sailed in search of Moby Dick. Month after month passed and the whale was not seen. Then one day, in the Great South Sea, Captain Ahab came up on to the deck at first light.

"What do you see?" he called to the look-outs.

"Nothing, sir!" came back from the men perched at the tops of the masts.

The captain tied about him the life-line which was used to haul him up to the main mast-head. In a moment he was on his way up to the top. When he was about two-thirds of the way up he peered into the distance, and suddenly raised a gull-like cry into the air, "There she blows! There she blows! A hump like a snow-hill! It is Moby Dick!"

His cry was taken up by the three look-outs. The men on deck rushed to the rigging to behold the famous whale they had so long been hunting. Ahab reached his final perch, some way below the other look-outs. From this height the whale was now seen some mile or so ahead. Every roll of the sea revealed his high sparkling hump, and the jet of water spouting high into the air.

"There she blows!" cried Ahab again. "Stand by to lower three boats. Keep her steady! Bring me down to the deck again! Quickly, quickly!"

"He's heading right away from us," shouted a look-out. "He cannot have seen the ship yet."

"Boats!" screamed Ahab. "Lower the boats!"

Soon the three boats had been lowered into the water and were being rowed in the direction of the unsuspecting white whale. Ahab sat quivering in the prow of the leading boat.

Like hollow shells the light craft sped through the sea, but only slowly neared the whale. The ocean grew more smooth, as if a carpet were being spread over the waves.

Before long, the white whale was clearly visible, his hump sliding along the sea, set in a revolving ring of green foam. Slowly the fore part of the great beast rose out of the water, forming a large arch, like some enormous bridge. It hung there for a moment, and then the white whale dived and was gone from view.

"We'll wait an hour," gritted Ahab.

"The birds! – the birds!" cried one of the rowers.

A long line of white sea-birds seemed to be flying directly to the boat containing Ahab. Their sight was keener than that of the sailors'. As Ahab peered down into the water he saw a white spot, no bigger than a weasel. Then two long crooked rows of white teeth began to float up from the bottom.

It was Moby Dick's open mouth, his vast bulk still half-blending with the blue of the sea. The glittering mouth yawned beneath the boat. Giving one sweep with his steering oar Ahab whirred the craft aside. Then he called to one of the seamen to take his place in the prow. Picking up a harpoon, the captain poised himself to strike when the whale appeared.

By spinning the boat Ahab had hoped to avoid the whale as it surfaced. But Moby Dick was as quick and as intelligent as any man, and much stronger. The great whale changed direction while still coming up, and placed itself beneath the craft again.

It came up just in front of the prow, its mouth open like a gigantic shark. Slowly the whale took the bow of the boat in its mouth and began to shake it.

The seamen left their oars and fled to the stern. A second later Moby Dick had bitten the boat completely in half! Ahab and the others were spilled out into the sea.

Moby Dick swam swiftly round and round the wrecked crew, churning the water in his wake, as if lashing himself up to still another and more deadly assault. The sight of the splintered boat seemed to madden him, and the sailors clinging to the wreckage wondered if their end had come.

The men remaining on board *Pequod* had seen what was happening from the ship's mast-heads. Swiftly they sailed the whaler towards the struggling sailors.

"Sail on the whale!" shouted Captain Ahab. "Drive him off!"

The *Pequod's* prows were pointed, and the vessel headed for the white whale. Reluctantly Moby Dick turned and swam off. As he did so, the boats flew to the rescue.

Ahab was dragged over the side of one of the craft. He pulled himself upright, demanding: "The harpoon – is it safe?"

"Aye, sir!"

"Any missing men?"

"One, two, three, four, five; – there were five oars, sir, and here are five men."

"That's good. Which way is the whale swimming?"

Moby Dick was now making good speed. The only hope of catching up with the whale lay in the *Pequod*. The two boats and the remains of the third were hauled on board. Hoisting every inch of sail, the *Pequod* bore down after Moby Dick.

"There she blows!" came a cry from the mast-head.

The thirty men on board the *Pequod* worked as one, just as the ship which carried them was one vessel although made of many different things – oak and maple, and pine wood; iron, and pitch, and hemp. All these things ran into each other in the one solid hull, which shot on its way like a cannon-ball.

The rigging lived. The mast-heads, like the tops of tall palms, were tufted with arms and legs. Clinging to a spar with one hand, some reached forth the other with impatient wavings; others, shading their eyes from the vivid sunlight, sat far out on the rocking sails. Ah, how they tried to seek out the thing that might destroy them!

"Lower the boats!" ordered Ahab at last.

Once more the ship's boats were swung out and lowered into the sea. Captain Ahab was about to descend into the leading one, when he turned to Starbuck, the mate.

"I am old," he said. "Shake hands with me, man."

Their hands and eyes met. "Oh, my captain, my captain, do not go," begged the mate.

"Lower away!" cried Ahab, tossing the mate's arm from him. "Stand by, the crew!"

In an instant the boat was pulling round close under the stern. Numbers of sharks rose out of the dark waters beneath the hull, snapping at the blades of the oars, every time they dipped into the water. The men strained their eyes. Moby Dick had dived beneath the surface again.

Suddenly the waters around them slowly swelled in broad circles. A low rumbling sound was heard and then a vast form shot out of the sea. The waters flashed like heaps of fountains, then sank in a shower of flakes.

"Give way!" cried Ahab to the oarsmen, and the boats darted forward to the attack. Moby Dick came forward in his turn, churning his tail among the boats; and once more flailed them apart. He spilled out the harpoons and lances from the two mates' boats, and dashed in one side of the upper part of their bows, but left Ahab's almost without a scar.

"Head for the whale!" cried Ahab again.

The seamen rowed their craft alongside the flank of Moby Dick. Soon they were within the smoky mountain mist thrown off from the whale's spout. Ahab balanced himself and hurled his lance into the beast's side, cursing fiercely.

Moby Dick crashed against the boat, writhing in agony. Ahab clutched the side, but three of the oarsmen were dashed into the water. Two managed to clamber back in, but the third was swept away.

For a moment it seemed as if the white whale would crush the small boat, but then Moby Dick caught a glimpse of the much larger *Pequod* and headed for that instead. He bore down on it, smiting his jaws amid fiery showers of foam.

From the ship's bows, nearly all the seamen hung, watching the approaching whale. Then the solid white wall of its forehead smote the ship's starboard bow. Men and timbers reeled. Some fell flat on their faces. The side of the ship splintered and water poured in.

Diving beneath the sinking ship, the whale ran quivering along its keel. It turned under the water and swiftly came to the surface again, and lay within a few yards of Ahab's boat.

Captain Ahab poised himself and flung yet another harpoon with deadly power at the beast.

The lance flew out, taking with it a long line. Moby Dick shuddered as the harpoon sank deeply into its body, killing it. In its death-throes the beast gave one last heave. The force of its pull took Captain Ahab over the side, to join the great white whale in death.

"The ship! Look at the ship!" screamed one of the remaining oarsmen.

The seamen turned and gazed across the sea. Only the uppermost masts of the *Pequod* were visible above the water. As they watched in horror, even these vanished beneath the waves.

IT WAS DREADFUL IN THE FOREST

from "The Lost World"
by Sir Arthur Conan Doyle

When I tell men that for a time I lived in a world of great prehistoric monsters, they do not believe me. And when I say that one of these beasts chased and hunted me down, they think I am mad.

But it is true, every word of it. It happened only a few years ago. My companions and I stumbled across this amazing lost world. It was as if time there had stood still. Nothing had changed since the dawn of time.

Great winged creatures swooped from the sky. Dinosaurs as big as houses roamed over the land, crushing trees beneath the weight of their feet. The plains and forests of this strange world were full of other huge beasts which men thought had died out thousands of years ago.

We found this fantastic world, my friends and I, in South America. It was thousands of miles up the great Amazon river, where no white men had ventured before.

I was the youngest of a small party of explorers. Over those amazing months we shared many dangers and adventures. Perhaps the most hair-raising was one encounter I had on my own.

We had made camp for the night in a large, dense forest. I could not sleep, and being young was not satisfied to lie staring up at the branches above me. I decided to explore a little on my own. I crept away from my companions as they snored in their sleeping bags next to the fire.

I had not gone more than a hundred metres before I was sorry. It was lonely in that great forest, and I did not know what lay before me. But I did not care to go back. Suppose one of my friends woke up and saw me? I would seem a fool for going out and a coward for coming back.

I pressed on with faltering footsteps. It was dreadful in the forest. The towering trees grew so thickly and their leaves and branches spread so widely that for long periods I could not see the moon above. Then suddenly it would shine through a gap and bathe the ground in a silvery light. Nervously I cradled my rifle in my arms and picked my way over the roots and mounds on the floor of the forest.

For a long time I saw no sign of any living thing, although I could hear many signs of them somewhere out in the darkness. After a while I came across a stream and began to follow its course. This in turn led me across a swamp. Here I came across the first of the great creatures I was to meet to my cost that night.

A great beast with wings, looking for all the world like a flying
skeleton, rose up before me and soared through the air. I froze
where I was, not daring to move. The creature flew into the trees
and then returned and settled with a great beating of wings, sinking
into its resting place in the swamp.

My heart was beating fast with the shock of this unexpected
meeting, but I forced myself to move on. The night was growing
still as the occupants of the forest settled to their rest. As I
advanced, however, I became aware of a low, rumbling sound. This
grew louder as I went on. Soon it was quite close to me. It was like
a boiling kettle or the bubbling from some great pot.

Soon I came across its source. In the centre of a small clearing I
found a lake of some black, pitch-like stuff. Its surface rose and fell
in great blisters of bursting gas. The ground round about was so hot
I could hardly bear to place my hand on it.

I had seen similar pools on my travels. Usually they were to be
found on the slopes of craters. The horrible thought came to me that
in addition to the rest of our perils we might be climbing the slopes
of a volcano on our voyage of discovery. Were this to be true, and
should the volcano explode there would be no hope for us.

I decided to hurry back to the camp and inform my companions of my find. It was a fearsome walk, and one which will be with me as long as my memory holds. In the great moonlit clearings I slunk along among the shadows on the edge. In the forest I crept forward, stopping with a beating heart if I heard, as I often did, the crash of breaking branches as some wild beast went past.

Now and then great shadows loomed up for an instant and were gone – great silent shadows which seemed to prowl upon padded feet. At last I saw the gleam of water amid the openings of the forest. Ten minutes later I was among the reeds upon the borders of the lake I had seen the day before.

I lay down and drank deeply. There was a broad path with many tracks upon it at the spot which I had found. It was clearly one of the drinking places of the animals. Close to the water's edge there was a huge flat rock. Up this I climbed and, lying on the top, I had an excellent view in every direction.

The lake lay like a sheet of quicksilver before me. The reflected moon shone brightly in the centre of it. It was shallow, for in many places I saw sandbanks poking above the water. On the still surface I could see signs of life. Upon a yellow sandbank I saw a creature like a huge swan, with a clumsy body and a high neck. Then it dived into the water, and I saw it no more.

Beneath me two creatures like enormous lizards had come down to the water to drink. They were squatting at the edge of the water, their long tongues like red ribbons shooting in and out as they lapped.

A huge deer with branching horns came down with its doe and two fawns. No such deer exists anywhere else on earth, for the biggest moose I have ever seen on earth would hardly have reached the shoulders of the one drinking at the lake.

Suddenly the great deer gave a warning snort and was off with its family among the reeds. The two great lizards also scuttled for shelter. A new-comer, a most monstrous animal, was coming down the path.

For a moment I wondered where I could have seen such an ungainly shape. The beast had an arched back, with triangular fringes along it, and a strange bird-like head held close to the ground. Behind it, dragging heavily over the ground, was an enormous tail. Great spikes of bone were attached to this tail, while slabs of bone covered the creature's body, almost like armour.

I wondered why I seemed to know such a fearful creature. Then it came to me. I had seen many drawings of the beast in books on dinosaurs, the creatures that walked the earth long before man appeared. This particular one was a stegosaurus.

The ground shook beneath his tremendous weight. His gulpings of water resounded through the still night. For five minutes he was so close to my rock that by stretching out my hand I could have touched his back. Then he lumbered away and was lost among the trees and rocks.

Looking at my watch, I saw that it was half-past two in the morning, and high time that I got back to the camp. I set out to retrace my path along the side of the brook.

I was in high spirits. I felt that I had done good work and was taking back good news to my companions. I could tell the others that the lake was full of strange creatures, and that I had seen several land animals which men believed to have been extinct for thousands of years. I thought as I walked that few men in the world could have spent a stranger night.

I was plodding up the slope, turning these thoughts over in my mind, when I heard a noise behind me. It was something between a snore and a growl, low, deep and very menacing. Some strange creature was evidently near me. Nothing could be seen, so I hurried on my way.

I had not gone far when the sound was repeated. It was still behind me, but louder and more menacing than before. My heart stood still within me as it flashed across me that this beast must surely be after *me*. My skin grew cold and my hair rose at the thought.

With my knees shaking beneath me I stood and glared with staring eyes down the moonlit path which lay behind me. All was quiet as in a dream landscape. Silver clearings and the black patches of bushes – nothing else could I see. Then from out of the silence there came once more that low, throaty croaking, far louder and closer than before. There could no longer be a doubt. Something was on my trail, and it was closing in upon me every minute.

I stood still, staring back. Then I saw it. There was movement among the bushes near the far end of the clearing I had just come across. A great dark shadow appeared and hopped out into the clear moonlight.

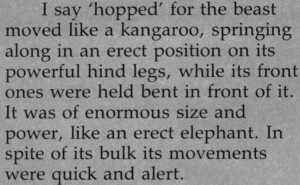

I say 'hopped' for the beast moved like a kangaroo, springing along in an erect position on its powerful hind legs, while its front ones were held bent in front of it. It was of enormous size and power, like an erect elephant. In spite of its bulk its movements were quick and alert.

His ferocious cry and horrible energy both assured me that this was one of the great flesh-eating dinosaurs, the most terrible beasts which have ever walked the earth.

As the huge brute lopped along it dropped forward upon its forepaws and brought its nose to the ground every twenty metres or so. It was smelling out my trail. Sometimes, for an instant, it was at fault. Then it would catch up again and come bounding swiftly along the path I had taken.

Even now when I think of that nightmare the sweat breaks out upon my brow. What could I do? My useless rifle was in my hand. What help could I get from that. I looked round for some rock or tree, but I was in a bushy forest with nothing higher than a sapling in sight.

I knew that the creature behind me could tear down a tree as though it were a reed. My only possible chance lay in flight. I could not move swiftly over the rough, broken ground, but as I looked round me in despair I saw a well-marked, hard-beaten path which ran across in front of me. I had seen such paths before. They were the runs of wild beasts, worn down over the years.

Flinging away my gun, I set out to run faster than I had ever done before. My limbs ached, my chest heaved, I felt that my throat would burst for want of air. Yet with that horror behind me I ran and ran and ran.

At last I stopped, hardly able to move. For a moment I thought that I had thrown him off. The path lay still behind me. And then suddenly, with a crashing and a thudding of giant feet and a panting of monster lungs, the beast was upon me once more. He was at my very heels. I was lost.

Now he had actually seen me. I started running again. The beast came after me in great bounds. The moonlight shone upon his huge projecting eyes, the row of enormous teeth in his open mouth, and the gleaming fringe of claws upon his short powerful forearms.

With a scream of terror I turned and rushed wildly down the path. Behind me the thick, gasping breathing of the creature sounded louder and louder. His heavy footfall was beside me. Every instant I expected to feel his grip upon my back. And then suddenly there came a crash – I was falling through space, and everything beyond was darkness and rest.

When I came round I was aware of a most dreadful smell. Putting out my hand in the darkness, I came across something which felt like a huge lump of meat. Up above me there was a circle of starlit sky. I seemed to be lying at the bottom of a deep pit. Slowly I staggered to my feet and felt myself all over. I was stiff and sore from head to foot, but I did not seem to have broken anything.

Then I remembered what had caused my fall. I looked up in terror, expecting to see the dreadful head of the monster peering down at me. There was no sign of the beast, however, nor could I hear any sound from above. I began to feel my way around in an attempt to find out where I was.

I was in a pit with sharply sloping walls and a level bottom about seven metres across. This bottom was littered with great pieces of flesh. After tripping and stumbling over them, I came across something hard. I found that an upright post was firmly fixed in the centre of the hollow. It was so high that I could not reach the top of it with my hand. It appeared to be covered with grease.

I remembered that I had a box of matches in my pocket. I struck one of them. Then I realised where I was. I was in a trap, one made by the hand of man. The post in the centre was about three metres long. It was sharp at the upper end, and it was black with the stale blood of creatures who had been impaled upon it.

The remains scattered about the ground were fragments of the victims, which had been cut away in order to clear the stake for the next who might blunder in.

It was clear that there were people living in this lost world. In order to get meat they dug pits like this one, with great spears stuck in the bottom. They dug these pits across the paths made by animals, and covered the holes with branches and leaves, so that the beasts would fall into the pit, as I had. It was only by the mercy of God that I had missed the sharpened stake and fallen straight to the ground.

The sloping pit would not be difficult for me to climb, but how did I know that the dreadful creature was not waiting for me in the nearest clump of bushes? I remembered reading somewhere that the dinosaurs, although large of frame, had very small brains. They could not reason things out.

If this should be true, then the beast which had been chasing me would not have the intelligence to wait and see if I appeared again. It was a chance I had to take.

Slowly I climbed to the top of the pit. I poked my head up and looked round. The stars were fading, the sky was getting lighter, and the cold wind of morning blew pleasantly upon my face. I could see or hear nothing of my enemy.

Slowly I climbed out and sat for a while upon the ground, ready to spring back into the pit if any danger should appear. After a while I plucked up my courage and stole back along the path which I had come. Some way down it I picked up my gun. Soon afterwards I found the brook which was my guide. So, with many a frightened backward glance, I made for home.

MR TOAD

by Kenneth Grahame

The animal friends of Mr Toad were very worried about him. Toad had gone mad over motor cars—buying them, driving them, and crashing them. For his own good he had to be made to stop. One fine morning, Rat, Mole and Mr Badger went to Toad Hall to talk to their friend.

They reached the drive of Toad Hall to find a shiny new motor-car of great size standing in front of the house. As they neared the door it was flung open, and Mr Toad, wearing goggles, cap, gaiters, and an enormous overcoat, came swaggering down the steps, drawing on his gloves.

"Hullo! come on, you fellows," he cried cheerfully. "You're just in time to come with me for a jolly—to come for a jolly—for a—er—jolly."

His hearty accent died away as he noticed the stern unbending looks on the faces of all his silent friends.

The Badger strode up the steps. "Take him inside," he said sternly.

"Now then," he said to the Toad, when the four of them stood together in the hall, "first of all, take those ridiculous things off!"

"Shan't!" replied Toad with great spirit.

"You two, take them off him," ordered Badger briefly.

They had to lay Toad out on the floor, kicking and calling all sorts of names, before they could get to work properly. Then the Rat sat on him, and the Mole took his motor-clothes off him bit by bit, and they stood him up on his legs again.

"You knew it must come to this, sooner or later, Toad," the Badger said sternly. "You've paid no attention to our warnings; you've wasted the money your father left you on cars; and you're giving us animals a bad name by your furious driving, your smashes and your rows with the police. Come with me, I'm going to give you a good talking-to."

He took Toad firmly by the arm and led him into another room, and closed the door behind them.

"*That's* no good," scoffed the Rat. "*Talking* to Toad will never cure him. He'll *say* anything."

Through the closed door they could hear the drone of Badger's voice. Presently it was joined by sobs from Toad, who was a very soft-hearted fellow.

After some three-quarters of an hour, the door opened and the Badger appeared, leading by the paw a very limp and sad-looking Toad.

"I'm pleased to say," announced the Badger, "that Toad has seen the error of his ways. He has promised to give up motor-cars. Tell them, Toad."

There was a long pause. Toad looked this way and that, while the other animals waited in grave silence. At last he spoke.

"No!" he shouted. "I'm *not* sorry. In fact I promise that the very first motor-car I see, poop-poop! off I go in it!"

"Very well, then," said the Badger firmly. "Take him upstairs you two, and lock him in. We're going to stay at Toad Hall until Toad promises to give up cars. Rat, telephone the garage and tell them to collect that monster outside."

For days the anxious animals kept a watch over Toad, taking it in turn to go out. One morning it was Rat's turn to be in charge. Badger and Mole had gone for a walk and Rat took Toad's breakfast up to him on a tray. He was greeted by a moan from the occupant of the bed.

"What's the matter, Toad?" asked the Rat.

"Oh, Rat," whispered a sad little voice. "Please step round to the village as quickly as possible—even now it may be too late—and fetch the doctor."

"A doctor! Oh, he must really be bad," the worried Rat said to himself, as he hurried from the room, not forgetting to lock the door behind him, and he set off for the doctor's house in the next village.

As soon as he heard the key turn in the lock, Toad hopped lightly out of bed. He watched the Rat disappear down the drive. Then, laughing heartily, he dressed as quickly as possible in the smartest suit he could lay his hands on, filled his pockets with cash from a drawer, then next, knotting the sheets from his bed together, tying one end of this rope round the leg of his bed, he scrambled out, slid lightly to the ground, and, taking the opposite direction to the Rat, marched off happily, whistling a merry tune.

At first he took bypaths, crossed many fields, and changed his direction several times. When he felt sure that he had thrown off any pursuers, he almost danced along the road in his satisfaction and conceit.

"Smart piece of work that!" he remarked to himself, chuckling. "Brain against brute force—and brain came out on top—as it's bound to do. Poor old Ratty! My! Won't he catch it when the others get back!"

Full of conceited thoughts such as these, Toad strode along, his head in the air, till he reached a little town, where the sign of "The Red Lion", swinging across the road half-way down the main street, reminded him that he was hungry. He marched into the inn, ordered the best lunch that could be provided and sat down to eat it in the coffee-room.

He was about half-way through his meal when an only too familiar sound coming down the street made him start trembling all over. The poop-poop! drew nearer and nearer, the car could be heard to turn into the inn-yard and come to a stop; Toad had to hold on to the leg of the table to conceal his emotion. Presently the party entered the room, hungry and talkative, boasting about their car. Toad listened eagerly, all ears, for a time; at last he could stand it no longer. Unseen, he slipped out of the room, paid his bill at the bar, and as soon as he was outside walked round quietly to the inn-yard. "There can't be any harm," he said to himself, "in my only just *looking* at it!"

No one else was around. The car stood in the middle of the yard. Toad walked slowly round it.

"I wonder," he said to himself presently, "I wonder if this sort of car *starts* easily?"

Next moment, hardly knowing how it came about, he found he had hold of the handle and was turning it.

As the familiar sound broke forth, the old passion seized Toad and completely mastered him, body and soul. As if in a dream he found himself, somehow, seated in the driver's seat; as if in a dream, he pulled the lever and swung the car round the yard and out through the archway; and, as if in a dream he increased his pace.

As he leapt forth upon the highroad he only knew that he was Toad once more, Toad at his best and highest, Toad the terror, the Lord of the lone trail, before whom all must give way or be smitten down.

"To my mind," observed the Chairman of the Bench of Magistrates cheerfully, "the *only* difficulty that presents itself in this case is, how can we make it really hot for the rogue and ruffian we see cowering in the dock before us. Let me see, he has been found guilty, on the clearest evidence, first, of stealing a valuable motor-car; secondly, of driving to the public danger; and thirdly of gross impertinence to the rural police. Mr Clerk, will you tell us, please, what is the stiffest penalty we can impose for each of these offences? Without, of course, giving the prisoner the benefit of any doubt, because there isn't any."

The Clerk scratched his nose with his pen. "Some people would consider," he observed, "that stealing the motor-car was the worst offence; and so it is. But cheeking the police undoubtedly carries the severest penalty; and so it ought. Supposing you were to say twelve months for the theft, which is mild; and three years for the furious driving, which is lenient; and fifteen years for the cheek, which was pretty bad sort of cheek, judging by what we've heard—those figures tot up to nineteen years."

"First rate!" said the Chairman.

"So you had better make it a round twenty years and be on the safe side," ended the Clerk.

"An excellent suggestion!" said the Chairman approvingly. "Prisoner! Pull yourself together and try to stand up straight. It's going to be twenty years for you this time. And mind, if you appear before us again, upon any charge whatever, we shall have to deal with you very seriously!"

Then the brutal minions of the law fell upon the hapless Toad and dragged him from the Court House, through the streets to the dungeon that lay at the end of the town. There at last they paused, where an old jailer sat fingering a bunch of mighty keys.

"Oddsbodikins!" said the Sergeant of Police, taking off his helmet and wiping his forehead. "Rouse thee, old loon, and take over from us this vile Toad."

The jailer nodded grimly, laying his withered hand on the shoulder of the miserable Toad. The rusty key turned in the lock, the great door clanged behind them. Toad was a helpless prisoner in the remotest dungeon, of the best-guarded keep, of the stoutest castle in all the length and breadth of Merry England.

When Toad found himself imprisoned in the dungeon, he flung himself full length on the floor and shed bitter tears, and gave himself to dark despair.

With laments like these he passed his days and nights for several weeks, refusing all meals. His plight struck the heart of the jailer's daughter, a pleasant and good-hearted girl. She took it upon herself to persuade Toad to eat, and even, in the end, to talk to her about himself and his past.

The jailer's daughter grew very sorry for Toad, and thought it a great shame that a poor little animal should be locked away for what seemed to her a very trivial offence. One morning she said,

"Toad, just listen, please. I have an aunt who is a washerwoman."

"There, there," said Toad graciously, "never mind; think no more about it. *I* have several aunts who *ought* to be washerwomen."

"Do be quiet a minute, Toad," said the girl. "My aunt does the washing for all the prisoners in this castle. She takes out the washing on Monday morning, and brings it in on Friday evening. This is a Thursday. Now this is what I think: you're very rich, at least you're always telling me so, and she's very poor. I think if she was properly approached, you could come to some arrangement by which she would let you have her dress and bonnet and so on, and you could escape from the castle as the official washerwoman. What do you say?"

"You are a good, kind, clever girl," said Toad. "Introduce me to your aunt, if you will, and I am sure we can come to some arrangement."

Next evening the girl ushered her aunt in to Toad's cell, bearing his washing pinned up in a towel. She had been prepared beforehand for what was to happen, and the sight of a few gold pieces left on the table by Toad were enough to persuade her.

In return for his cash, Toad received a cotton print gown, an apron, a shawl, and a black bonnet. At the old lady's request, Toad gently gagged and bound her, and left her in a corner of the cell.

"Now it's your turn, Toad," said the jailer's daughter. "Take off that coat and waistcoat of yours; you're fat enough as it is."

Shaking with laughter, she dressed him in her aunt's clothes, finishing by tying the strings of her own bonnet under his chin.

"You're the very image of auntie," she giggled. "Now, goodbye Toad, and good luck. Go straight down the way you came up."

With a quaking heart Toad left the cell on his bid for freedom.

He was soon agreeably surprised to find how easy it was. The washerwoman was plainly a popular figure. Each warder passed on the figure in the print dress and the black bonnet, with a kind word to the next guardian of the prison.

It seemed hours to Toad before he crossed the last courtyard, rejected the pressing invitations from the last guardroom, and dodged the outspread arms of the last warder, pleading for just one last embrace. But at last he heard the gate close behind him, and knew that he was free!

Dizzy with success Toad walked towards the lights of the town, not knowing in the least what he would do next, but certain of one thing, that he must remove himself as quickly as possible from this area.

As he walked along, his attention was caught by some red and green lights a little way off to one side of the town, and the sound of the puffing and snorting of engines. "Aha!" he thought, "this is a piece of luck! A railway station is the thing I want most in the world at the moment."

He made his way to the station accordingly, looked at a time-table and found that a train bound, more or less in the direction of his home, was due to start in half an hour. "More luck!" said Toad, his spirits rising rapidly, and went off to the booking-office to buy his ticket.

He gave the name of the station nearest Toad Hall, and searched for the necessary money. But here the cotton gown intervened and prevented his reaching his pockets. In a sort of nightmare he struggled with the dress, while other would-be passengers lining up behind him made unkind and impatient remarks.

At last—somehow—he burst through to where his waistcoat pocket should be situated, only to remember that his waistcoat and his jacket, containing all his money, had been left behind in his cell.

In his misery he made one last effort to carry the thing off, and with a return to his fine old manner, he said, "Look here! I find I've left my purse behind. Just give me that ticket, will you, and I'll send the money on tomorrow. I'm well-known in these parts."

The clerk stared at him and the dusty black bonnet for a moment, and then laughed. "I should think you are pretty well known in these parts," he said, "if you've tried this game often. Here, stand away from the window, please, madam; you're in the way of the other passengers!"

An old gentleman who had been prodding him in the back for some moments thrust him away and, what was worse, addressed him as his good woman, which angered Toad more than anything else.

Baffled and full of despair, he wandered blindly down the platform to where the train was standing, and tears trickled down each side of his nose.

As he walked he found himself opposite the engine, which was being oiled and wiped by its driver, a burly man with an oil-can in one hand, and a lump of cotton-waste in the other.

"Hullo, mother!" said the engine-driver, "what's the trouble?"

"O sir!" said Toad, crying afresh. "I am a poor, unhappy washerwoman, and I've lost all my money, and can't pay for a ticket, and I *must* get home tonight somehow, and whatever I am to do I don't know. O dear, O dear!"

"That's a bad business, indeed," said the engine-driver slowly. "Lost your money—and can't get home—and got some kids waiting for you, I dare say?"

"Any amount of 'em," sobbed Toad. "And they'll be hungry—and playing with matches— and upsetting lamps, the little innocents!—and quarrelling, and going on generally. O dear, O dear!"

"Well, I'll tell you what I'll do," said the good engine-driver. "You're a washerwoman to your trade, says you. Very well, that's that. And I'm an engine-driver, as you may well see, and there's no denying it's terribly dirty work. Uses up a power of shirts, it does, till my missus is fair tired of washing 'em. If you'll wash a few shirts for me when you get home, and send 'em along, I'll give you a ride on my engine. It's against the rules, but we're not so very particular in these out-of-the-way parts."

The Toad's misery turned into rapture as he eagerly scrambled up into the cab of the engine. The guard waved his welcome flag, the engine driver whistled in cheerful response, and the train moved out of the station. As the speed increased, and the Toad could see real fields on either side of him, and trees and hedges, and cows and horses, all flying past him, he thought how every minute was bringing him nearer to Toad Hall.

THE STORY OF CALIPH STORK

by Andrew Lang

The Caliph, the chief man in all old Baghdad, was resting one afternoon. The Grand Vizier, his chief helper, came to see him.

"Why do you look so anxious, my friend?" asked the Caliph.

"Alas," said the Grand Vizier, "outside the palace is a pedlar. He is selling many beautiful things, but I have so little money to spare."

For some time the Caliph had wished to give his friend a present, so he sent a slave to fetch the pedlar before him. When the pedlar arrived, he turned out to be a short stout man in very ragged clothes. He carried a box with all manner of wares inside: strings of pearls, rings, combs and richly mounted pistols.

The Caliph and his Vizier inspected everything. The Caliph chose some handsome pistols for himself and for the Vizier. Just as the pedlar was about to close his box, the Caliph saw a small drawer. He asked the pedlar if he had anything else to spare for sale.

The pedlar opened the drawer and took out a box containing some black powder and a scroll written in strange characters, which neither the Caliph nor the Vizier could read.

"I got these two items from another merchant," he said. "I don't know what they are, but they are of no use to me. You may buy them if you like."

The Caliph bought the powder and the scroll, and sent the pedlar away. Then he asked the Vizier if he knew of anyone who could read the writing on the scroll.

"There is an old man called Selim in the city," said the Vizier. "He knows every language under the sun. I shall send for him."

When Selim arrived he studied the scroll. "My lord," he said, "it is written in Latin."

"Well, let us hear what it means," said the Caliph.

The old man began to read aloud from the scroll. "Anyone who sniffs the powder in this box, and at the same time says the word 'Mutabor!', can turn himself into any creature he likes. He will understand the language of all animals. When he wishes to become a human being again, he must bow three times to the east and repeat the same word. He must be careful, when he takes the shape of some bird or beast, not to laugh, or he would forget the magic word and remain an animal for ever."

The Caliph was delighted. He gave Selim a splendid robe and made him promise not to tell anyone about the magic powder. Then he sent the old man away.

"Tomorrow," the Caliph told the Vizier, "we will go into the country, sniff the powder, and then hear what is being said in air, earth and water."

The next morning, the Caliph and the Vizier walked with the box through the town to a pond far out in the country. There they saw a stork walking up and down, hunting for frogs. At the same time they saw another stork high in the sky, flying towards the same spot.

"Why don't we turn ourselves into storks? Then we could talk to those two," said the Vizier.

"That's a good idea," said the Caliph, "but let us remember how we are to turn ourselves back into men again. We must bow three times to the east, and say 'Mutabor!'. If we do that we will return to our human form. But for Heaven's sake don't laugh, or we are lost!"

The second stork circled and then landed. Quickly the Caliph took out the box and sniffed at the powder. Then he handed the box to the Vizier, who did the same. Finally the two men cried together 'Mutabor!'.

At once their legs grew thin and red; their smart yellow slippers turned to clumsy stork's feet; long necks sprouted between their shoulders; their beards disappeared, and their bodies were covered with feathers.

Meantime the second stork had reached the ground. It first scraped its bill with its claw, stroked down its feathers, and then walked towards the first stork. The Caliph and the Vizier, now storks themselves, drew closer and listened to the other two talking.

"Good morning, Dame Longlegs. You are out early this morning."

"Yes indeed, dear Chatterbill. I am getting myself a little breakfast. May I offer you a joint of lizard?"

"A thousand thanks, but I am here for something else. I am to dance tonight at a party, and I have come here for a little practice." The young stork began to move about with the most wonderful steps. The Caliph and the Vizier looked on. When the dancing stork suddenly balanced on one leg and flapped her wings up and down, they each burst out laughing.

"That's the funniest thing I've ever seen," said the Caliph, wiping the tears from his eyes.

Suddenly the Vizier remembered that they had been warned not to laugh. He reminded the Caliph of this.

"O dear!" said the Caliph, suddenly serious. "It would be dreadful if we had to remain storks for the rest of our days. Do try and remember the word we have to say. I have forgotten it!"

"We must bow three times to the east and say 'M . . . mu . . . mu . . .'."

They turned to the east and started bowing till their bills touched the ground, but, oh horror—the magic word was quite forgotten. No matter how hard they tried, they could not remember it. The Caliph and the Vizier remained storks as they were.

They wandered sadly across the fields. In their misery they could not think what to do next. For several days they wandered about, living on fruit. They found that they did not care much for frogs and lizards. Their one comfort was the power of flight, so often they flew over the roofs of Baghdad to see what was going on there.

During the first few days they saw signs of many disturbances in the streets below. Men were fighting and shouting. But about the fourth day, as they sat on the roof of the palace, they saw a splendid procession passing in the streets below them. Drums and trumpets sounded, a man in a scarlet and gold mantle sat on a great horse, surrounded by slaves. He was followed by soldiers who shouted, "Hail, Mirza, the Lord of Baghdad!"

"Now that I have gone, my greatest enemy has become ruler of Baghdad," groaned the Caliph.

"Let us fly to the sacred city of Medina," said the Vizier. "Perhaps we shall find help there."

They rose from the palace roof, and spread their wings towards Medina. But flying was not yet an easy matter for them, and they soon grew tired.

"Oh!" gasped the Vizier, after a couple of hours. "I can go on no longer; you fly too quickly for me. Let us find somewhere to spend the night."

In a valley below them they saw an old ruin. It had once been a castle, but now only a few rooms remained. The two storks walked along the corridors, seeking a dry spot. Suddenly the Vizier stopped.

"I heard someone close sigh and moan," he whispered.

"I heard it too," said the Caliph. "The sound came from down there."

They both hurried down a dark passage and stopped outside a door. From within the room behind the door they heard sighs mixed with sobs. The two storks opened the door and went in.

On the floor of the ruined room, lit by the moonlight streaming in through one small barred window, sat a huge screech owl. Big tears rolled from its large round eyes. When it saw the storks it gave a joyful cry. It gently wiped the tears from its eyes with spotted wings, and to the great amazement of the two visitors addressed them in the human tongue.

"Welcome, storks!" she croaked. "You have come to save me."

"Oh, screech owl," said the Caliph sadly, "it looks as if you have suffered in the same way we have. There is little that we can do to help anyone. Listen to our story."

In a few short sentences the Caliph told the owl how he and the Vizier had become storks. When he had finished the screech owl shook her head.

"My story is as sad as yours," she sighed. "I am the daughter of the King of the Indies. One day a wicked magician gave me a drink which changed me into an owl. That magician brought me to this horrible place, and told me that here I must stay until someone of his own free will asks me to marry him. Since then many months have passed and I have been forced to live here as an owl."

The Caliph fell into deep thought on hearing this story of the princess. "If I am not much mistaken," said he, "there is some connection between our misfortunes, but I do not know what."

"I think I know of a way in which we might save ourselves," said the owl excitedly. "Once a month the wicked magician who turned me into a bird comes to these ruins. Near here is a large hall in which he feasts with his companions. They tell each other all about their evil deeds. It is possible that they will mention the magic word which will turn you back into humans."

"Oh, dearest Princess," begged the Caliph, "tell me when he comes and where this hall is."

"Do not think me unkind," said the owl, "but I will do that on one condition. I want to be free too. One of you must offer to marry me."

The storks were rather taken aback by this. The Caliph and the Vizier went out of the room to talk together.

"Grand Vizier," said the Caliph, "this is a tiresome business. However, you can marry her."

"Oh yes, indeed?" answered the Vizier, "what do you think my wife would do if I took a princess home? She would scratch my eyes out. Besides, you are both young and unmarried."

They argued on for some time, but in the end when the Caliph saw that the Vizier would rather remain a stork to the end of his days than marry the owl, he agreed to propose to the bird himself. The owl was delighted. She told the two storks that the magician was due to arrive that very night.

She then led the Caliph and the Vizier to the hall. They passed through a long dark passage until a bright ray of light shone before them. The owl told her companions to keep very quiet.

Through a gap near where they stood, they could see the whole of the hall. It contained many fine pillars. In the middle of the hall stood a round table covered with dishes of food. Around the table sat eight men. One of them was the pedlar who had sold the Caliph the powder.

The man next to the pedlar begged him to tell of his latest doings. The pedlar then told the story of the Caliph and the Vizier.

"And what kind of word did you give them?" asked another of the wicked magicians at the table.

"An old Latin word; it is 'Mutabor'," said the pedlar.

As soon as the storks heard this they were overjoyed. They ran at a great pace to the door of the ruined castle. When they reached it the Caliph turned to the owl. "We are very grateful to you. Please take me as your husband."

Then he turned towards the east. Three times the storks bowed their heads to the sun, which was just rising over the mountains.

"Mutabor!" they both cried, and in an instant they were changed back into their old forms. The Caliph and the Grand Vizier fell weeping and laughing into each other's arms. Who shall describe their surprise when they turned round and saw standing before them a beautiful lady in a fine gown.

With a smile she held out her hand to the Caliph, and asked "Do you not recognise your screech owl?"

It was she! The Caliph was so enchanted by her grace and beauty, that he cried out that being turned into a stork had been the best piece of luck that had ever befallen him.

The three set out at once for Baghdad. The Caliph had enough gold in his purse to buy in the nearest village all that they needed for their journey. So at last they reached the gates of Baghdad.

Here the Caliph's arrival created a great sensation. His people had given him up for dead, and now they rejoiced to see their beloved ruler again.

The Caliph ruled long and happily with his wife the Princess. His merriest time was when the Grand Vizier visited him in the afternoon. When the Caliph was in high spirits he would imitate the Vizier's appearance when he was a stork. He would strut gravely with stiff legs up and down the room, chattering and showing how he had vainly bowed to the east and cried "Mu . . . Mu . . ."

The Caliph's wife and their children were always much entertained by this show, but if the Caliph carried on too long, the Vizier would take him to one side, and with a laugh threaten to tell the Caliph's wife how the Caliph had once tried to persuade the Grand Vizier to marry the screech owl instead!

BRER RABBIT AND BRER FOX

by Joel Chandler Harris

Brer Rabbit and Brer Fox lived with many other animals on a patch of countryside, where the sun was usually shining. These two animals did not like one another very much. They were always trying to play tricks on each other. Brer Fox was stronger than Brer Rabbit, but Brer Rabbit could think faster.

One day, a group of animals were clearing a patch of land to plant some crops. Brer Rabbit got very hot. He did not like to tell the others, in case they thought he was lazy, so he shouted out that he had got a thorn in his paw and would have to stop work for a while.

Quietly he slipped away, looking for somewhere cool to rest. After a while he came across a deep well, with a bucket hanging in it.

"That looks cool," said Brer Rabbit. "I'll just take a rest in that bucket."

With that he jumped into the bucket. At once the rope tied to the bucket began to unwind and the bucket went down into the well. Brer Rabbit was frightened. He knew where he came from, but he didn't know where he was going. Suddenly he felt the bucket hit the water. He sat very still, shaking and shivering in spite of himself.

Brer Fox had seen Brer Rabbit slip away and had followed him to see what he was up to now. He had watched while Brer Rabbit had jumped into the bucket and the bucket had descended into the well.

"Well, if that don't beat everything," said Brer Fox. "I reckon Brer Rabbit must keep his money hidden down in that well. Or maybe he's found a gold-mine. Anyway, I'm going to see for myself."

Brer Fox crept up closer to the well. Then he peered down into it. He couldn't see or hear anything. At the bottom of the well, Brer Rabbit was still too scared to move.

"Hey, Brer Rabbit!" called out Brer Fox. "I know you're down there. What are you doing?"

"Who? Me? Oh, I'm just fishing," called Brer Rabbit. "I was going to surprise you all by bringing a pile of fish back with me for our supper."

"Are there many down there, Brer Rabbit?"

"Lots of 'em, Brer Fox. The water's alive with fish. Come down and help me haul them in."

"How am I going to get down?" shouted Brer Fox.

"There's another bucket up there. It'll fetch you down all safe and sound."

Brer Rabbit sounded so happy that Brer Fox jumped into the other bucket. This bucket was tied to the other end of the rope which passed over a tree trunk above the top of the well. This meant that as the heavy Brer Fox went down, his weight pulled Brer Rabbit up.

When they passed each other at the half-way mark, Brer Rabbit sang out:

"Goodbye, Brer Fox, take care o' your clothes,
For this is the way the world goes;
Some goes up and some goes down,
You'll get to the bottom all safe and soun'."

As soon as Brer Rabbit got to the top of the well, he jumped out of the bucket and ran off to the farmer who owned the well, and told him that Brer Fox was down at the bottom, getting the water dirty. Then he hurried back to the well, and shouted down to Brer Fox:

"Here comes a man with a great big gun—
When he haul you up, you jump and run."

Brer Fox did just this, managing to run off into the trees before the farmer could shoot him when he pulled the bucket up. Before long, both animals were working back on the patch of ground again, just as if they had never heard of the well. But every now and then Brer Rabbit would burst out laughing, and Brer Fox would scowl and say nothing at all.

A day or two later, Brer Fox and Brer Bear were walking back from their gardens carrying some cabbages in two baskets. Who should they see but Brer Rabbit, asleep under a tree.

"I've got you this time!" shouted Brer Fox, and he jumped on Brer Rabbit and stuffed him into the pocket of his coat.

"What's happening?" squealed Brer Rabbit, waking up.

"I've caught you at last, that's what's happened," cried Brer Fox. "That'll teach you to go to sleep where I can find you."

"Let me out!" pleaded Brer Rabbit.

"You stay where you are, I've got plans for you," said Brer Fox, and he and Brer Bear went walking off together, carrying their baskets of cabbages.

It was not long before the two animals reached Brer Bear's house. The bear invited the fox in for a drink of honey-syrup. They went inside and put down their baskets.

Suddenly Brer Rabbit jumped out of Brer Fox's pocket, and went running round the room.

"You can run all you want to," sneered Brer Fox. "The doors and windows are shut. I'll find you wherever you go."

Without a word Brer Rabbit ran under the bed. There was a mat there. He scurried underneath it and lay still, his heart pumping.

"Is that the best you can do?" laughed Brer Fox, peering under the bed. "I can see your hump in that mat. You stay there till I'm ready for you."

Brer Rabbit still said nothing. He stayed under the mat until he heard Brer Bear pouring Brer Fox his drink. Then he wriggled out from under the mat and looked all about him.

On the other side of the bed were Brer Bear's slippers. Brer Rabbit took these in his mouth and slipped them under the mat. Then he sat back and looked at the hump they made. It looked as if he was still hiding under the mat himself!

Brer Rabbit smiled contentedly. It looked as if he was going to fool that old fox yet again. Quietly he crept towards the basket of cabbages that Brer Fox had left in a corner. While Brer Fox was talking to Brer Bear the rabbit crept into the basket and hid himself under the cabbages.

"Keep an eye on that rabbit under the carpet," he heard the fox say to the bear. "I'll just take my cabbages back home and put them in the stewpot. Then I'll come back and we can prepare ourselves a nice rabbit pie!"

With that Brer Fox picked up his basket of cabbages and carried his burden out of the house, and through the wood on the way to his home. He had not gone very far when Brer Rabbit gave a great groan in the bottom of the basket.

"Oooooh!" he moaned. "Ooooooh!"

"My goodness!" said Brer Fox, stopping and looking round in alarm. "What was that?"

"Oooooooh!" groaned Brer Rabbit again, now enjoying himself.

"It sounds as if it's coming from my basket," quavered a terrified Brer Fox. "I'm carrying some talking cabbages!"

"Ooooooh!" said Brer Rabbit as loudly as he could. "Put me down!"

"It is the cabbages!" shouted Brer Fox, dropping the basket with a thump.

Quickly Brer Rabbit punched two holes in one of the cabbage leaves and pushed his two eyes through them, glaring at the shaking Brer Fox. The fox screamed and jumped in the air.

"Those cabbages don't only talk, they've got eyes!" he screamed, and turned and ran off as fast as he could.

Brer Rabbit waited until the fox had reached the end of the track, then he came out from behind the cabbage leaf and called after the other animal. Brer Fox stopped and turned round. His jaw dropped open when he saw Brer Rabbit waving casually at him.

"Thanks for the ride, old friend," called out the rabbit, and picking up one of the cabbages for his lunch he disappeared among the trees, leaving Brer Fox behind him.

Brer Fox decided that it was time he got his own back on Brer Rabbit, so he set out to make a fool of him. He got some tar and turpentine and mixed it together. From this mixture he made a Tar Baby, a life-sized, black doll that was very sticky.

Brer Fox took the Tar Baby out into the road and placed it there. Then he went and hid in the bushes, where he could see what would happen.

It was not long before Brer Rabbit came hopping down the road. Brer Fox lay low. Brer Rabbit pranced along until he saw the Tar Baby. Then he reared up on his hind legs in astonishment. Brer Fox still lay low.

"Good morning," said Brer Rabbit to the Tar Baby. "Nice weather we're having."

The Tar Baby said nothing, and Brer Fox lay low.

"How are you feeling today?" went on the rabbit.

Still the Tar Baby said nothing. Brer Rabbit began to get cross.

"Are you deaf?" he asked sharply. "'Cause if you are, I can shout, you know."

The Tar Baby did not move, and Brer Fox lay low.

"You're stuck up, that's what you are," decided Brer Rabbit. "Think you're too good for me, huh? I'm going to cure that!"

Brer Fox chuckled to himself, but the Tar Baby said nothing, and did not move.

"I'm going to teach you how to meet respectable folk," said Brer Rabbit. "I'm going to do that if it's the last thing I do. If you don't take off your hat and say 'Howdy!', I'm going to bust you wide open."

The Tar Baby did not move, and Brer Fox lay low in the bushes, trying not to laugh.

Brer Rabbit kept on asking the Tar Baby to speak to him, and the Tar Baby said nothing. In the end Brer Rabbit got so wild that he drew back his fist and hit the Tar Baby on the side of the head. His fist stuck fast there and he could not pull it free.

"If you don't let go of me, I'll hit you again!" shouted Brer Rabbit. With that he hit the Tar Baby on the other side of the head with his other fist. That stuck there as well, and Brer Rabbit could not pull his fists away from the tar.

"Turn me loose, or I'll kick the stuffing out of you!" shouted Brer Rabbit, but the Tar Baby stood still and said nothing.

Brer Rabbit kicked out with both feet. They stuck to the Tar Baby as well. Then Brer Rabbit said that if the Tar Baby did not let him go he would butt him with his head. The Tar Baby stood still, so Brer Rabbit hit him with his head. That got stuck too!

Just then Brer Fox sauntered casually out of the bushes.

"Hi there, Brer Rabbit," he said. "You look kind of stuck-up this morning!"

Then Brer Fox rolled on the ground and laughed and laughed until he could laugh no more.

THE TIGER

by William Blake

Tiger! Tiger! burning bright
In the forests of the night,
What immortal hand or eye
Could frame thy fearful symmetry?

In what distant deeps or skies
Burnt the fire of thine eyes?
On what wings dare he aspire?
What the hand dare seize the fire?

And what shoulder, and what art,
Could twist the sinews of thy heart?
And when thy heart began to beat,
What dread hand? and what dread feet?

What the hammer? what the chain?
In what furnace was thy brain?
What the anvil? what dread grasp
Dare its deadly terrors grasp?

Then the stars threw down their spears
And watered heaven with their tears,
Did he smile his work to see?
Did he who made the Lamb make thee?

Tiger? Tiger? burning bright
In the forests of the night,
What immortal hand or eye
Dare frame thy fearful symmetry?

THE RELUCTANT DRAGON

by Kenneth Grahame

Hundreds of years ago there was a dragon who hated fighting. He let all the fighting dragons get on with it and went to live in a cave near a village. He spent all his time there writing poems and playing with his young friend, the Boy.

One day a stranger rode into the village. When the Boy found out who he was, he ran up the hill to the cave.

"It's all up, Dragon!" he shouted, as soon as he was within sight of the beast. "He's coming! He's here now! You'll have to pull yourself together and do something at last!"

The dragon was licking his scales and rubbing them with a bit of cloth the Boy's mother had lent him, till he shone like a great green jewel.

"Who's coming, Boy?" he yawned, without looking round.

"It's only St George who's coming, that's all," panted the Boy. "He's got the longest, wickedest-looking spear you ever did see. And it's his job to fight dragons, and kill 'em." And the Boy began to jump around in sheer delight at the prospect of this battle.

"O deary, deary me," moaned the dragon, "this is too awful. I won't see him, and that's flat. I don't want to know the fellow at all. You must tell him to go away at once, please."

"Now Dragon, Dragon," begged the Boy. "You've *got* to fight him some time or other, you know, 'cos he's St George and you're the dragon. Better get it over with."

"My dear little man," said the dragon, "just understand once and for all that I can't fight and I won't fight. I've never fought in my life, and I'm not going to start now."

"But if you don't fight he'll cut your head off," gasped the Boy, miserable at the prospect of losing both his fight and his friend.

"Oh, I think not," said the dragon in his lazy way. "You'll be able to arrange something. I've every confidence in you, you're such a *manager*. Just run down to the village, there's a good chap, and make it all right. I leave it entirely to you."

The Boy made his way back to the village. He entered the inn and went through to the room where St George sat.

"May I come in, St George?" said the Boy politely, as he paused at the door. "I want to talk to you about the dragon."

"Yes, come in, Boy," said the Saint kindly. "Another tale of misery and wrong, is it? Whom do you want avenged?"

"Nobody," said the Boy quickly. "The fact is, this is a *good* dragon."

"What do you mean?" frowned the Saint.

"Well, he's a friend of mine, and tells me the most beautiful stories you ever heard, all about the old times and when he was little. And he's kind. He's as engaging and as trustful and as simple as a child."

"I see," mused St George. "Perhaps I've misjudged the animal. But what are we to do?"

"I suppose you couldn't go away quietly, could you?" asked the Boy hopefully.

"Impossible, I fear," said the Saint. "Quite against the rules."

"Well then, look here," said the Boy. "Would you mind strolling up with me and seeing the dragon and talking it over. It's not far, and any friend of mine will be welcome."

"Well, it's irregular," frowned the Saint, "but it does seem sensible. All right, I'll come and talk to your dragon."

"I've brought a friend to see you, Dragon," said the Boy loudly.

The dragon woke up with a start. "I was just-er-thinking about things," he said in his simple way. "Very pleased to meet you, sir."

"This is St George," said the Boy shortly. "St George—the dragon."

"Don't you think," said St George in his pleasant way, "that the best plan would be just to fight it out? After all, I could make you."

"No, you couldn't," said the dragon firmly. "I should only go into my cave and hide down the hole in there. You'd soon get sick of hanging about waiting for me to come and fight."

St George gazed for a while at the fair plain around them. "This would be a great place for a fight," he sighed.

"But you see, I don't like fighting," explained the dragon.

"Then why don't we pretend to fight?" suggested the Saint. "I could spear you somewhere it wouldn't hurt, and that would be that."

"Could you do that?" asked the dragon, suddenly interested.

"Oh yes, there's such a lot of you that there must be a few spare places somewhere. Under the neck, for example—all those thick folds of skin. I could spear you there, and that would be that."

"Then what would happen?" asked the dragon.

"Well, according to the rules I should lead you in triumph to the village."

"And then?"

"Oh, there'll be shouting and speeches and things."

"Quite so," said the dragon. "And then?"

"Oh, and then," said St George, "why, and then there will be the usual feast, I suppose."

"Good," said the dragon, "and that's where *I* come in. Look here, I'm bored to death up here. I shall meet a lot of people at this feast. They'll see what a fine chap I am. I shall make a lot of friends. Very well, St George, the fight is on!"

St George and the Boy walked back down the hill. Suddenly the Saint stopped.

"*Knew* I'd forgotten something," he said. "There ought to be a Princess. Terror-stricken and chained to a rock, and all that sort of thing. Boy, can't you arrange a Princess?"

The Boy was in the middle of a great yawn. "I'm tired to death," he wailed, "and I *can't* arrange a Princess, or anything more, at this time of night. Anyway, my mother's sitting up for me, and *do* stop asking me to arrange things till tomorrow!"

Next morning, at quite an early hour, large numbers of people began streaming up to the Downs. They were dressed in their Sunday clothes and carried baskets of food and drink.

The Boy had a good front place, well up towards the cave. He was feeling anxious. Could the dragon be depended upon? He might change his mind and stay inside.

St George's red plumes topped the hill, as the Saint rode slowly forth to a great level place in front of the cave. Very gallant and beautiful he looked on his tall war-horse, his golden armour glancing in the sun, his great spear held erect, the little white pennon, crimson-crossed, fluttering at its point. He drew rein and waited.

"Now then, Dragon," muttered the Boy.

A low muttering, mingled with snorts, now made itself heard, rising to a bellowing roar that seemed to fill the plain. Then a cloud of smoke hid the mouth of the cave. Out of the midst of it the dragon himself, shining, magnificent, pranced forth.

Everybody said "oo-oo-oo!" as if he had been a mighty rocket. His scales were glittering, his long spiky tail lashed his sides, his claws tore up the turf and sent it flying over his back, and smoke and fire jetted from his nostrils.

"Oh, well done, Dragon!" cried the Boy. "Didn't think he had it in him," he added to himself.

St George lowered his spear, bent his head, dug his heels into his horse's side, and came thundering over the turf. The dragon charged with a roar and a squeal.

"Missed!" yelled the crowd. There was a moments tangle of golden armour and blue-green coils and spiky tail, and then the great horse, tearing at his bit, carried the Saint, his spear swung high in the air, almost up to the mouth of the cave.

The dragon sat down and barked viciously. St George pulled his horse round into position.

"End of Round One!" thought the Boy. "How well they managed it! But I hope the Saint won't get excited. I can trust the dragon all right. What a play-actor the fellow is."

St George managed to get his horse to stand steady, and was looking round him as he wiped his brow. Catching sight of the Boy, he smiled and nodded and held up three fingers for an instant.

"It all seems to be planned out," said the Boy to himself. "Round Three is to be the last one. Wish it could have lasted a bit longer. What's that old fool of a dragon doing now?"

The dragon was showing off, running round and round in circles, sending waves and ripples of movement along his spine, from his pointed ears right down to the spike at the end of his long tail.

St George gathered up his reins and began to move forward, dropping the point of his spear and settling himself in his saddle.

"Time!" yelled everybody excitedly.

The dragon sat up on end and began to leap from one side to the other. This made the horse swerve. The Saint only just saved himself by the mane; and as they shot past, the dragon delivered a vicious snap at the horse's tail which sent the poor beast running madly far over the Downs.

The crowd began to cheer the dragon, who strutted to and fro, his chest thrust out and his tail in the air, enjoying his new popularity.

St George had dismounted and was telling his horse exactly what he thought of him. The Boy made his way down to the Saint and held his spear for him.

"It's been a jolly fight, St George!" he said, with a sigh. "Can't you let it last a bit longer?"

"Well, I think I'd better not," said the Saint. "The fact is, your simple old friend's getting conceited now they're cheering him. He'll forget about our arrangement and start playing the fool. Then there's no telling where he would stop. I'll just finish him off in this round."

He swung himself into his saddle and took his spear from the Boy. "Now don't you worry," he said kindly. "I've marked the spot exactly, and the dragon's bound to help, because he wants to go to the feast."

St George trotted smartly towards the dragon and circled round him. The dragon did the same, circling round the Saint. So the two waited for an opening, while the spectators watched in breathless silence.

There was a sudden movement of the Saint's arm, and then a whirl of confusion of spines, claws, tail, and flying bits of turf. The dust cleared away, the spectators whooped and ran in cheering. The Boy saw that the dragon was down, pinned to the earth by the spear, while St George had got off his horse and was standing over him.

It all seemed so real that the Boy ran up, hoping the dear old dragon wasn't hurt. As he approached, the dragon lifted one large eyelid, winked, and collapsed again. He was held fast to the earth by the neck, but the Saint had hit him in the spare place agreed upon, and it didn't even seem to tickle.

"Ain't you going to cut 'is 'ed orf, master?" asked one of the crowd. He had bet on the dragon to win, and was feeling a little sore.

"Well, not *today*, I think," said St George pleasantly. "You see, that can be done at *any* time. There's no hurry at all. I'll give him a good talking-to, but first I think we should all go down to the village and have some refreshment."

At that magic word *refreshment* the whole crowd lined up and waited for the signal to start. St George hauled on his spear with both hands and released the dragon. The dragon rose and shook himself and ran his eye over his spikes and scales and things to see that they were all in order. Then the Saint mounted and led everyone down the hill to the village. The dragon followed meekly behind with the Boy.

There were great doings when they got to the village again. St George made a speech in front of the inn. He told the crowd that he had tamed the dragon for them, and the dragon was willing to settle down and be a friend to everyone, so *they* must all make friends with *him* as well.

Then the Saint sat down amid great cheers. The dragon nudged the Boy in the ribs and told him that he couldn't have done it better himself. Then everyone went off to get ready for the feast.

It turned out to be a most pleasant affair. St George was happy because there had been a fight and he hadn't had to kill anybody. The dragon was happy because there had been a fight, and so far from being hurt in it, he had become very popular. The Boy was happy because there had been a fight and in spite of it, both his two friends were on the best of terms. And all the others were happy because there had been a fight, and—well—they didn't need any other reason for their happiness.

At last the feast was over, the guests had left, and only St George, the Boy and the dragon were left. The dragon had fallen asleep over the table.

"Come on, Dragon," said St George firmly. "The Boy is waiting to take you home, and so am I."

They woke the dragon and set off up the hill arm-in-arm, the Saint, the dragon and the Boy. The lights in the little village began to go out; but there were stars and a late moon, as they climbed to the Downs together. As they turned the last corner and disappeared from view, snatches of an old song were carried back on the night breeze. I can't be certain which of them was singing, but I *think* it was the dragon.

THE BLIND CAT AND THE LAME FOX

by Carlo Collodi

Pinocchio was a puppet made of wood. He had a long nose and he could run and jump as well as any boy. He dearly wanted to be a boy, and he was as naughty as any child. He ran away from the man who had carved him, and had many adventures. At the end of them he had managed to save five gold pieces. He decided that he had had enough of wandering and that he would go back home.

He had not gone far when he met two strange creatures on the road. There was a fox who was lame in one foot, and a cat who was blind. They helped each other along. The fox leaned on the cat and told her which way to go.

"Where are you going?" asked the fox pleasantly.

"I'm going home," Pinocchio told the two animals proudly. "I'm rich; I've got five gold pieces."

He showed them the money. The fox's lame paw reached out, and the cat's eyes opened wide for a moment, but Pinocchio did not notice.

"Pray, what will you do with all that money?" asked the fox.

"I shall buy a beautiful new coat for the man who made me," said Pinocchio, "and then I shall buy myself a book, so that I can go to school and learn things."

"You don't want to do that," said the cat at once. "Learning things can be very bad for you."

A bird which was singing in a hedge suddenly stopped warbling and said, "Pinocchio, don't listen to these two bad animals!"

In one swift movement the cat had jumped on the bird and had eaten it. Then quickly she closed her eyes and pretended to be blind again.

"What did you do that for?" asked Pinocchio.

"To teach him a lesson," said the cat. "Birds should not interrupt when their betters are talking."

"Talking of money," said the fox, "would you like to make yours much bigger?"

"How could I do that?" asked Pinocchio.

"We know a special place," said the cat.

"It's called the Field of Miracles," said the fox. "Anyone who has a gold piece may bury it there and leave it. During the night a tree of gold pieces will sprout up from where the one gold piece is buried."

"Really?" asked the astounded Pinocchio. "Suppose I buried my five gold pieces? How many would I get in return?"

"Thousands," said the cat. "Simply thousands."

"That's marvellous!" shouted Pinocchio. "Please take me there. If you do, I'll give you a present of some of the gold pieces that grow on the trees there."

"Certainly not!" said the cat offended.

"We wouldn't dream of taking a present from you," said the fox.

"We shall take you to the Field of Miracles because we like you," said the cat. "Come this way."

The three of them walked a long way for the rest of the day. Just as night was falling they came across an inn and decided to spend the night there. They entered the inn and had a good meal, and then went to their rooms to sleep.

Pinocchio did not have a good night. He kept dreaming about trees growing in fields, and each tree bearing many gold pieces, instead of leaves.

He woke up very early, while it was still dark, and went down the stairs to the inn.

"Are my friends up yet?" he asked the landlord.

"Up and left," said the man. "They didn't want to disturb you, so they said they would wait for you at the Field of Miracles. It's straight across the fields opposite the inn."

"Did they pay the bill?" yawned Pinocchio.

"Oh no! To do so would have been an insult to you. That's one gold piece, please."

Pinocchio gave up one of his pieces of gold and went outside. It was very dark and he had to feel his way across the fields. Only a few birds swooped in front of him and then were gone again.

For an hour or so Pinocchio made his way slowly in the direction of the Field of Miracles. He was passing a small clump of trees when two figures leapt out on him. They were both wrapped in charcoal sacks. It seemed to Pinocchio that the figures were oddly familiar, but he could not remember where he had seen them before. Quickly he placed his four remaining pieces of gold under his tongue.

"Your money or your life!" demanded the taller of the two figures, seizing Pinocchio.

The puppet made signs with his hands, as if to say, "I have no money!"

"Give up your money, or we'll kill you!" said the second figure, in a voice Pinocchio had heard somewhere else.

The puppet opened his mouth to plead for his life. As he did so the coins beneath his tongue chinked.

"So you've hidden your money in your mouth!" cried the taller of the two figures. "Spit it out!"

Pinocchio shook his head stubbornly. The second figure took out a knife and tried to force it between the puppet's lips. Pinocchio suddenly opened his mouth and bit off the figure's hand. He spat it out. To his surprise he saw that it was the paw of a cat that was lying on the ground.

The cat screamed. Pinocchio jumped over a hedge and ran for his life. His two attackers raced after him, although the cat who had lost a paw was forced to hobble badly.

They ran for what seemed a long time through the dark. Pinocchio could not shake the other two off. Finally in desperation, he climbed a tall pine tree and perched in its topmost branches. The two figures clad in sacks tried to climb after him, but kept slipping back down again. Then they lit a fire at the base of the tree and kept throwing dry sticks on to it. Soon the tree was blazing fiercely. Pinocchio jumped down and set off across the fields again. His two attackers kept doggedly after him.

Dawn was beginning to break when Pinocchio stumbled across a wide ditch full of dirty water. He hesitated. What could he do? Another minute and the other two would be upon him. The puppet braced himself.

"One, two, three!" he cried, and with a great effort cleared the ditch.

He turned and looked back. His pursuers were dithering on the far side of the ditch. As Pinocchio stared at them they made up their minds. Both sack-clad figures dashed at the water and tried to leap across the ditch. Each fell short and descended into the water with a splash! Pinocchio laughed.

"Enjoy your bath!" he shouted, and trotted off.

Soon it was daylight. Pinocchio slowed down to a walk. He began to pass people as he strolled across the fields. He was safe enough now. He made his way to a road and walked along it.

As he was passing a big oak tree, he heard someone moving in the bushes at the side of the road. Pinocchio stopped. After a moment the fox and the cat appeared. Both looked very clean, as if they had had a good wash.

"Dear Pinocchio," shouted the fox, kissing the puppet. "What are you doing here?"

"Oh, it's a long story," said Pinocchio. "Early this morning I was attacked by two robbers. They wanted to take my gold coins from me."

"Never!" exclaimed the cat. "Aren't some people wicked!"

"Anyway, I managed to escape, so that's all right," said the puppet. Suddenly he saw that the cat seemed lame, with one paw missing. "What happened to your paw?" he asked.

The cat looked confused, but the fox answered quickly. "Dear old cat," he said fondly, "she's so generous. Give anyone anything, she will. Why, back down the road we met an old wolf, starving to death. Quick as you like, my friend here bit off her paw and gave it to the poor fellow for breakfast. She's like that, she is."

"Never mind that," growled the cat. "It's lucky we met you, Pinocchio. The Field of Miracles isn't very far away. We can be there in half an hour. Come on!"

The three of them walked on down the road. Before long they came to a town.

125

"What do they call this place?" asked the puppet curiously.

"Er, Fools' Trap," said the fox. "I can't think why," he added.

Pinocchio glanced from side to side as they walked through the streets of the town. It really did seem a most unusual place. Almost everyone in it seemed to be suffering in some way. The dogs had lost their coats and the sheep their fleeces, and were shivering with the cold. Butterflies had sold their wings and were walking; peacocks were without their tails, and pheasants had lost their lovely feathers.

The only inhabitants who seemed to be happy were a few foxes being driven past in great coaches, and a magpie or two being carried by footmen through the streets.

The lame fox and the blind cat took Pinocchio through the town, and out of its boundaries to a field. It seemed just like every other field that the puppet had ever seen.

"Here we are," said the cat impatiently. "This is the Field of Miracles. Dig a small hole with your hands and put your four gold coins in it."

Pinocchio did as he was told. He dug the hole, put in the gold pieces, and covered them over with earth.

"Now you must bring some water from the special stream over there," said the fox, "and sprinkle it over the earth."

Pinocchio carried the water in his shoe from the stream and poured it over the hole he had dug.

"What should I do next?" he asked when he had finished.

"That's all," said the fox. "Now we must all go away. If you come back on your own in about twenty minutes, you will find four trees bearing many gold coins growing where you have dug your hole. No, no, we want no thanks. It has been a pleasure to know you, Pinocchio."

126

The fox and the cat went off in one direction, while Pinocchio wandered off the other way, back into the city. Soon he was out of sight of the field. His mind was full of great fancies as he tried to make up his mind what he would buy with his new wealth. Only when he was quite sure that twenty minutes had passed did the puppet turn and make his way back to the Field of Miracles.

To his amazement there were no trees growing where he had planted his four gold pieces. Pinocchio waited impatiently, in case he had come back too soon. Still nothing happened. With a sinking heart the puppet realised that something had gone wrong. Wondering what had caused the delay he started to dig up the earth. There was no sign of his money. He dug deeper and harder. Still there was nothing there, not even his four gold coins.

A great screech of laughter came from a tree above him. The puppet glared up to see an old parrot cleaning the few feathers it had left.

"What are you laughing at?" demanded Pinocchio, trembling with anxiety.

"I am laughing because you have been cheated," answered the parrot boldly, "just as I was cheated when first I came to Fools' Trap."

"Cheated?" asked Pinocchio in dismay. "How have I been cheated?"

"While you were away," chuckled the parrot, "the fox and the cat came back and dug up your four gold pieces. They will be far away by now, and you will never catch them up."

Pinocchio turned back to the hole at his feet. He dug deeper and deeper and deeper. Soon there was a great cavern yawning at his feet, but no gold pieces.

The puppet climbed back up to the field and ran off to the town as fast as his legs would carry him.

There he lost no time reporting to the judge in the court house that he had been cheated out of his money. The judge listened kindly to all that the puppet had to tell him. When Pinocchio had finished his sorry tale the judge rang a bell at his side.

At once two great mastiffs dressed as policemen appeared in the doorway.

"Another poor fool complaining," said the judge in a bored tone.

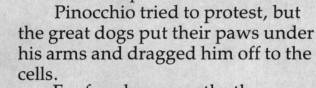

"Take him to prison at once."

Pinocchio tried to protest, but the great dogs put their paws under his arms and dragged him off to the cells.

For four long months the puppet remained in prison. Then he had a stroke of luck. The King of Fools' Trap won a great battle. To celebrate, he ordered that all the rascals in the town's prison be set free.

One by one the other prisoners were released until only the puppet remained in the cells.

"Why haven't I been allowed to go, too?" asked Pinocchio.

"I'm afraid that only rascals are to be set free," said the jailer. "You claim to be an honest fellow."

"No, no, I'm a rascal, I'm a rascal!" cried Pinocchio quickly.

"In that case," said the jailer, bowing low, "please permit me to escort you from the prison."

Once he was out of the cells, Pinocchio ran and ran until the town of Fools' Trap was far behind him. It began to rain and soon the road was very muddy, but still the puppet did not slow down.

"What a fool I've been," said Pinocchio to himself, as he hurried down the road. "I've deserved everything that's happened to me. I've been as obstinate as a mule, I've been selfish, and I've never listened to good advice. But that's all behind me now. If only I'm allowed to reach home safely, I'll be a different puppet. I'll be good, obedient and loving, I promise I will!"

The words were hardly out of his mouth when he stopped and jumped back in fright. Stretched across the road in front of him was a great serpent. Its skin was green, its eyes were red and from its tail poured clouds of smoke.

Pinocchio waited, hoping that the serpent would move on, but the great beast stayed where it was. In the end the puppet summoned up his courage and walked towards it.

"Excuse me, sir," he said respectfully, "I would like to go home. It's been such a long time since I was there. Do you think you could move just a little, so that I could pass?"

The serpent did not answer. Pinocchio thought perhaps it was asleep. He walked back a little and then ran forward to leap over the great beast. Just as he did so the serpent raised its head to strike the puppet. In his fright Pinocchio overbalanced and fell backwards. His head got stuck in the mud and his legs waved wildly in the air.

The sight of Pinocchio looking so ridiculous made the serpent laugh so heartily that it could not strike at the puppet. Instead it laughed and laughed so much that suddenly it choked. At the same time a blood vessel burst in its heart, killing the serpent.

Pinocchio climbed over the dead body and set off running towards his home.

"Perhaps my luck is beginning to change for the better," he said as he went.

THE WATER BABIES

by Charles Kingsley

Although he was only a boy, Tom had been a chimney sweep. He had the hard and dangerous job of climbing up narrow chimneys with his brushes. Then he was changed. A fairy turned him into a water-baby, just a few centimetres long, who could spend all his time swimming at the bottom of rivers.

Tom loved his new life in the water. Sometimes he went along the smooth gravel waterways, looking at the crickets which ran in and out among the pebbles. Then he would swim into the great water forests. There were water flowers there in their thousands. Tom tried to pick them: but as soon as he touched them, they drew themselves in and turned into knots of jelly; and then Tom saw that they were all alive—bells, and stars, and wheels of all shapes and colours.

The water-baby soon learned the language of the creatures living in the water, and was able to talk to them. One day he came across a great ugly creature sitting just under the bank of the river. It was about half as big as himself, with six legs and a great stomach, and a most ridiculous head with two great eyes and a face just like a donkey's.

"Oh," said Tom, "you are an ugly fellow, to be sure!" and he began making faces at him.

Suddenly a long arm with a pair of pincers on the end shot out and caught Tom by the nose. It did not hurt him much; but held him quite tight.

"Yah, ah! Oh, let me go!" cried Tom.

"Then leave me alone," said the creature. "I want to split."

"Why do you want to split?" asked Tom, rubbing his nose when it was released.

"Because my brothers and my sisters have all split, and turned into beautiful creatures with wings; and I want to split too. Don't speak to me. I am sure I shall split. I will split!"

Tom stood still and watched him. And the creature swelled himself, and puffed, and stretched himself out stiff, and at last—crack, puff, bang—he opened up all down his back, and then up to the top of his head.

And out of his inside came the most slender, elegant, soft creature as soft and smooth as Tom: but very pale and weak, like a little child who had been ill a long time in a dark room. Then it began walking slowly up a grass stem to the top of the water.

Tom was so astonished that he said not a word: but he stared wide-eyed. Then he went up to the top of the water too, and peeped out to see what would happen.

As the creature sat in the warm sun, a wonderful change came over it. It grew strong and firm; the most lovely colours began to show on its body, blue, yellow, black, and spots, bars and rings. Out of its back rose four great wings of bright brown gauze. Its eyes grew so large that they filled all its head, and shone like ten thousand diamonds.

"Oh, you beautiful creature!" said Tom; and he put out his hand to catch it.

But the thing whirled up into the air, and hung poised on its wings for a moment, and looked down at Tom.

"No," it said, "you cannot catch me. I am a dragon-fly now, the king of all the flies. I shall dance in the sunshine, catch gnats, and have a beautiful wife like myself. Goodbye!"

Tom watched the dragon-fly fluttering over the river until it disappeared from sight. Then he dived back down to the bottom. He found himself in the middle of a shoal of trout, and swam along with them. As they leapt out of the water to catch flies, so Tom jumped too.

Presently it came on to rain. Then the thunder roared, and the lightning flashed, till the rocks in the stream seemed to shake. Tom looked up at the storm above through the water, and thought it the finest thing he had ever seen in his life.

The rain poured into the river, causing it to rise higher and higher and rush along at a great rate, full of beetles, sticks, straws, worms, wood-lice and leeches.

Tom could hardly stand against the power of the stream, and hid behind a rock. But the trout did not. Out they rushed from among the stones and began gobbling the beetles and leeches.

By flashes of lightning, Tom saw a great new sight—all the bottom of the river alive with great eels, turning and twisting along and away. They had been hiding for weeks past in the cracks of the rocks. As they hurried past Tom could hear them say to each other, "We must run, we must run. What a jolly thunderstorm! Down to the sea, down to the sea!"

Then the otter came by with all her brood, sweeping along as fast as the eels themselves. She spied Tom as she came by, and said: "Now is your time, if you want to see the world. Come along, children, never mind those nasty eels. We shall breakfast on salmon tomorrow. Down to the sea, down to the sea!"

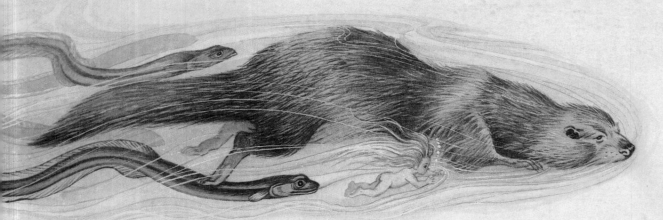

Tom needed no more invitation. He followed the others in the great rush to the sea. On and on he went in that great floating procession; on through narrow passages and great roaring waterfalls; past sleeping villages and under great bridges, away and away to the sea. And when daylight came, he was there, at the mouth of the great river where it joined the ocean. Tom felt a little frightened.

"What a great wide place it is," he said to himself. "If I go into it I shall surely lose my way."

So he went back a little way and slept in the crack of a rock. When he awoke it was light and the river was calm again as it flowed into the great sea. Then Tom saw a sight which made him jump up.

Such a fish! ten times as big as the biggest trout, and a hundred times as big as Tom, sculling up the river. It was shining silver from head to tail, with here and there a crimson dot; a grand hooked nose and a curling lip. As Tom looked on, it leapt high out of the water and over a rock. The water-baby knew that this must be a salmon, the king of fish.

Slowly and carefully Tom swam out into the wide sea. He passed shoals of bass and mullet, leaping and rushing after shrimps; and once he passed a huge shining seal.

"How do you do, sir?" piped Tom. "What a beautiful place the sea is!"

Instead of trying to bite him, the seal looked at Tom with his soft, sleepy, winking eyes, and said, "Good tide to you, my little man!"

Tom went on, calling out cheerful greetings to fleets of purple sea-snails and a shoal of porpoises, all smooth and shining as if they had been polished. Then he swam in towards the shore, and before long he was among the rocks in the shallow water off the beach. He chatted idly to the barnacles clinging to the rocks, and then turned a corner. Suddenly he saw a sort of cage ahead of him. Inside it was a sad-looking lobster, twiddling with his horns instead of thumbs.

"Hello," said Tom. "Have you been naughty and been put in a lock-up?"

"I can't get out," groaned the lobster.

"The point is," said Tom, "how did you get in there in the first place?"

"Don't you know what this is?" demanded the lobster. "This is a lobster-pot, left among the rocks by fishermen to catch creatures like me. Before long, a man will come by, open the pot, and take me home for his supper."

"Oh dear," said Tom thoughtfully. "We can't have that."

"I just can't get out," said the lobster. "I've jumped upwards, downwards, backwards, and sideways at least four thousand times; I always end up back here. I can't find the hole I came in through. There are great spikes in here, so if I move about too much, I'll tear myself on them."

Tom looked at the trap carefully, and thought he saw a way of freeing the prisoner.

"Turn your tail up to me," he said, "and I'll pull you through, and you won't stick on the spikes."

But the lobster was so stupid and clumsy that he couldn't reach the hole. Tom reached down till he grasped the lobster. Then the clumsy creature pulled him into the trap head-first.

"This is a pretty fix!" said the water-baby. "Never mind, I can see a way out. Take your great claws and break the points of these spikes. Then we can get up to the hole and go out through it."

"Dear me," said the lobster, "I never thought of that."

In no time at all he had broken off the spikes in the lobster pot. The lobster and Tom swam out through the hole and made their escape hastily.

"Much obliged," nodded the lobster, hurrying off across the rocks. "I hope I can do you a favour some time."

"Think nothing of it," called out Tom, and he dived back into the water.

THE COWARDLY LION

by Frank Baum

Dorothy had been an ordinary girl living on a farm in Kansas in the USA. In a great storm she had been knocked senseless.

When she came round she found that she was no longer on the farm. Instead she was in the strange land of Oz. A Good Witch told her that if she wanted to get back home to Kansas again, she would have to follow the yellow brick road to the Emerald City, where she would find the marvellous Wizard of Oz.

The brave girl set out on her long journey, her little dog Toto by her side. On the way, Dorothy made two friends who decided to go with her to see the Wizard. The stuffed Scarecrow thought that he would ask the Wizard for some brains, while the Tin Woodman, who was always getting rusty, said that he would ask the Wizard for a heart.

They walked through thick woods. The road was still paved with yellow bricks, but these were almost covered with dried branches and dead leaves, and the walking was not at all good.

There were few birds in this part of the forest, for birds love the open country where there is plenty of sunshine. But now and then there came a deep growl from some wild animal hidden among the trees. These sounds made the little girl's heart beat fast, for she did not know what made them; but Toto knew, and he walked close to Dorothy's side, and did not even bark in return.

"How long will it be?" the child asked of the Tin Woodman, "before we are out of the forest?"

"I cannot tell," was the answer, "for I have never been to the Emerald City. My father told me once that it was a long journey through dangerous countryside."

Just as he spoke there came from the forest a terrible roar, and the next moment a great Lion bounded into the road. With one blow of his paw he sent the Scarecrow spinning over and over to the edge of the road, and then he struck at the Tin Woodman with his sharp claws. But, to the Lion's surprise, he could make no impression on the tin, although the Woodman fell over in the road and lay still.

Little Toto, now that he had an enemy to face, ran barking towards the Lion, and the great beast opened his mouth to bite the dog, but Dorothy, fearing Toto would be killed, rushed forward and slapped the Lion upon his nose as hard as she could, while she cried out:

"Don't you dare to bite Toto! You ought to be ashamed of yourself, a big beast like you, to bite a poor little dog!"

"I didn't bite him," said the Lion, as he rubbed his nose with his paw where Dorothy had hit it.

"No, but you tried to," she said sharply. "You are nothing but a big coward."

"I know it," said the Lion, hanging his head in shame. "I've always known it. But how can I help it?"

"I don't know, I'm sure. To think of your striking a stuffed man, like the poor Scarecrow!"

"Is he stuffed?" asked the Lion in surprise, while he watched her pick up the Scarecrow, set him upon his feet, and pat him into shape again.

"Of course he's stuffed," replied Dorothy, who was still angry.

"That's why he went over so easily," remarked the Lion. "It astonished me to see him whirl around so. Is the other one stuffed also?"

"No," said Dorothy, "he's made of tin." She helped the Woodman up again.

"That's why he nearly blunted my claws," said the Lion. "When they scratched against the tin it made a cold shiver run down my back. What is that little animal you are so careful of?"

"He is my dog, Toto."

"Is he made of tin, or stuffed?"

"Neither. He's a—a—a meat dog," said the girl.

"Oh! He's a curious animal and now that I look at him, seems remarkably small. No one would think of biting such a little thing except a coward like me," said the Lion sadly.

"What makes you a coward?" asked Dorothy, looking at the great beast in wonder, for he was as big as a small horse.

"It is a mystery," replied the Lion. "I suppose I was born that way. All the other animals in the forest naturally expect me to be brave, for the Lion is thought to be the King of the Beasts. I learned that if I roared very loudly every living thing was frightened and got out of my way. Whenever I've met a man, I've been scared. But I've just roared at him, and he has always ran away as fast as he could go. But really I'm very frightened myself."

"Most peculiar," said Dorothy.

"Anyway, where are you all going?" asked the Lion.

"I'm going to the Wizard of Oz to ask for some brains, for my head is stuffed with straw," said the Scarecrow.

"And I'm going to ask him to give me a heart," said the Tin Woodman.

"And I'm going to ask him to send Toto and me back to Kansas," said Dorothy.

"Then if you don't mind," said the Lion, "I'll come with you and ask the Wizard to give me some courage."

"You will be very welcome," said Dorothy.

So once more the little company set off upon the journey, the Lion walking with stately strides at the girl's side. For a time it was a quiet journey, marred only when the Tin Woodman stepped upon a beetle. This upset the Woodman and made him cry. The tears ran slowly down his face and over the hinges of his jaw, and there they rusted. When Dorothy asked him a question, the Tin Woodman could not open his mouth, for his jaws were rusted together. The Scarecrow seized the oil-can from Dorothy's basket and oiled the Woodman's jaws, so that after a few moments he could talk as well as before.

"That will teach me to look where I step," he said. "For if I should kill another bug or beetle I should surely cry again, and crying rusts my jaws so that I cannot speak."

Before long they came across a great ditch that crossed the road and divided the forest as far as they could see on either side. It was a very wide ditch, and when they crept up to the edge and looked into it they could see that it was also very deep, and there were many big, jagged rocks at the bottom. The sides were so steep that none of them could climb down. For a moment it seemed that their journey must end.

"What shall we do?" asked Dorothy in despair.

"I think I could jump over it," said the Lion slowly.

"Then we are all right," said the Scarecrow, "for you can carry us all over on your back, one at a time."

"Well, I'll try it," said the Lion. "Who will go first?"

"I will," declared the Scarecrow, "for, if you found that you could not jump over the gulf, Dorothy would be killed, or the Tin Woodman badly dented on the rocks below. But if I am on your back it will not matter so much, for the fall would not hurt me at all."

"I am terribly afraid myself of falling," said the Cowardly Lion, "but I suppose there is nothing to do but try it. Get on my back."

The Scarecrow sat on the Lion's back. The big beast walked to the edge of the ditch and crouched down. Then giving a great spring, he shot through the air and landed safely on the other side. They were all greatly pleased to see how easily he did it, and after the Scarecrow had got down from his back, the Lion sprang across the ditch again.

Dorothy thought she would go next. So she took Toto in her arms and climbed on the Lion's back, holding tightly to his mane with one hand. The next moment it seemed as if she were flying through the air; and then, before she had time to think about it, she was safe on the other side. The Lion went back a third time and got the Tin Woodman, and then they all sat down for a while to give the beast a rest.

They found the forest very thick on this side, and it looked dark and gloomy. After the Lion had rested they started along the road of yellow brick, silently wondering, each in his own mind, if ever they would come to the end of the woods and reach the bright sunshine again. To add to their discomfort, they soon heard strange noises in the depths of the forest, and the Lion whispered to them that it was in this part of the country that the Kalidahs lived.

"What are Kalidahs?" asked the girl.

"They are monstrous beasts with bodies like bears and heads like tigers," replied the Lion, "and with claws so long and sharp that they could tear me in two as easily as I could kill Toto. I'm terribly afraid of the Kalidahs."

"I'm not surprised that you are," agreed Dorothy. "They must be dreadful beasts."

The Lion was about to reply, when suddenly they came to another gulf across the road. But this one was so broad and deep that the Lion knew at once he could not leap across it.

So they sat down to consider what they should do. After serious thought the Scarecrow said, "Here is a great tree, standing close to the ditch. If the Tin Woodman can chop it down, so that it will fall to the other side, we can walk across it easily."

"That is a first-rate idea," said the Lion. "One would almost suspect you had brains in your head, instead of straw."

The Woodman set to work at once, and so sharp was his axe that the tree was soon nearly chopped through. Then the Lion put his strong front legs against the tree and pushed with all his might. Slowly the big tree tipped and fell with a crash across the ditch, with its top branches on the other side.

They had just started to cross this queer bridge when a sharp growl made them all look up. To their horror they saw running toward them two great beasts with bodies like bears and heads like tigers.

"They are the Kalidahs!" said the Cowardly Lion, beginning to tremble.

"Quick!" cried the Scarecrow. "Let us cross over."

So Dorothy went first, holding Toto in her arms. The Tin Woodman followed, and the Scarecrow came next. The Lion, although he was certainly afraid, turned to face the Kalidahs. Then he gave so loud and terrible a roar that Dorothy screamed and the Scarecrow fell over backward. Even the fierce beasts stopped short and looked at him in surprise.

But, seeing that they were bigger than the Lion, and remembering that there were two of them and only one of him, the Kalidahs again rushed forward. The Lion crossed over the tree and turned to see what they would do next. Without stopping an instant the fierce beasts also began to cross the tree. And the Lion said to Dorothy, ''We are lost, for they will surely tear us to pieces with their sharp claws. But stand close behind me, and I will fight them as long as I am alive.''

''Wait a minute!'' called the Scarecrow. He had been thinking what was best to be done. Now he asked the Woodman to chop away the end of the tree that rested on their side of the ditch. The Tin Woodman began to use his axe at once. Just as the two Kalidahs were nearly across, the tree fell with a crash into the gulf, carrying the ugly, snarling brutes with it, and both were dashed to pieces on the sharp rocks at the bottom.

''Well,'' said the Cowardly Lion, drawing a long breath of relief. ''I see we are going to live a little while longer.''

The little group hurried on. Towards the end of the afternoon the trees became thinner, and they suddenly came upon a broad river, flowing swiftly just before them. On the other side of the water they could see the road of yellow brick running through a beautiful country, with green fields dotted with bright flowers and all the road bordered with trees hanging full of delicious fruits.

''How shall we cross the river?'' Dorothy asked.

''The Tin Woodman must build us a raft, so that we may float to the other side,'' said the Scarecrow.

So the Woodman took his axe and began to chop down small trees to make a raft, while Dorothy found a pleasant spot under a tree and sat down and closed her eyes. Soon she was dreaming of the Emerald City, and of the Wizard of Oz, who would soon send her back to her own home again.

THE HAPPY PRINCE

by Oscar Wilde

High above the city, on a tall column, stood the statue of the Happy Prince. He was gilded all over with thin leaves of fine gold, for eyes he had two bright sapphires, and a large red ruby glowed on his sword-hilt.

One night there flew over the city a little Swallow. His friends had flown south to the warm lands six weeks before, but he was late and was hurrying to get away before it grew too cold.

He saw the statue on the tall column and decided to spend the night in its shelter. He was about to go to sleep between the statue's feet when a large drop of water fell on him.

The bird looked up and saw that the eyes of the Happy Prince were filled with tears. They were running down his golden cheeks and falling to the ground.

"Why are you crying?" asked the Swallow.

"It is because I can see all the ugliness and misery of the city from up here," said the statue. "Although my heart is only made of lead, I must weep."

"What can you see that makes you so sad?" asked the bird.

"In a little street," said the Prince, "there is a poor house. One of the windows is open. I can see a woman sitting at a table. She is poor and hungry. In a bed in a corner of the room her little boy is lying ill. He has a fever, and he is asking for oranges. His mother has nothing to give him but river-water. Swallow, will you take her the ruby from my sword-hilt? She can sell it and buy food. My feet are fixed to the ground, so I cannot go myself."

"My friends are waiting for me in the warm lands," said the Swallow.

"Stay one night and be my messenger," begged the Happy Prince.

The statue looked so sad that the little Swallow was sorry. "It is very cold here," he said, "but I will stay with you for one night, and be your messenger."

"Thank you, little Swallow," said the Prince.

So the bird picked out the great ruby from the Prince's sword, and flew away with it in his beak over the roofs of the town. At last he

came to the poor house and looked in. The boy was lying on his bed, and his mother had fallen asleep, she was so tired.

In hopped the bird, and laid the great ruby on the table by the woman's head. Then he flew gently round the room, fanning the boy's forehead with his wings. "How cool I feel," said the boy. "I must be getting better," and he sank into a deep sleep.

Then the Swallow flew back to the Happy Prince, and told him what he had done.

"It is curious," he remarked, "but I feel quite warm now, although it is so cold."

"That is because you have done a good deed," said the statue. And the little Swallow began to think, and then he fell asleep. Thinking always made him sleepy.

When day broke, he flew down to the river and had a bath. Then he went back to the Happy Prince.

"I am just off to the warm lands," he chirped.

"Swallow, Swallow, little Swallow," said the statue, "will you not stay with me one night longer?"

"My friends are waiting for me in the warm lands," said the bird.

"Swallow," said the Happy Prince, "far away across the city I see a young man in a tiny room. He is leaning over a desk covered with papers. He is trying to finish writing a play, but he is too cold to write any more. There is no fire in the grate, and hunger has made him faint."

143

"I will wait with you one night longer," said the Swallow, who really had a good heart. "Shall I take him another ruby?"

"Alas! I have no ruby now," said the Prince. "My eyes are all I have left. Pluck one of them out and take it to him. He will sell it, and buy firewood, and finish his play."

"Dear Prince," said the Swallow, "I cannot do that," and he began to weep.

"Swallow, Swallow, little Swallow," said the Happy Prince, "do as I ask you."

So the Swallow plucked out the Prince's eye, and flew away to the writer's room. It was easy enough to get in, as there was a hole in the roof. Through this he darted, and came into the room. The young man had his head buried in his hands, so he did not hear the flutter of the bird's wings. When he looked up he found the beautiful jewel at his side.

"This must be from some great admirer!" he cried. "Now I can finish my play!"

The next day the Swallow flew down to the harbour. He sat on the mast of a large vessel and watched the sailors. "I am going to the warm lands," he cried, but nobody minded, and when the moon rose he flew back to the Happy Prince.

"I have come to say goodbye," he cried.

"Swallow, Swallow, little Swallow," said the Prince, "will you not stay with me one night longer?"

"It is winter," replied the bird, "and the chill snow will soon be here. I must leave you, but I will never forget you."

"In the square below," said the Happy Prince, "there is a little girl selling matches. She has let her matches fall in the gutter, and they are all spoiled. Her father will beat her if she does not bring home some money, and she is crying. She has no shoes or stockings, and her little head is bare. Pluck out my other eye, and give it to her, and her father will not beat her."

"I will stay with you one night longer," said the Swallow, "but I cannot pluck out your eye. You would be quite blind then."

"Swallow, Swallow, little Swallow," said the Prince, "do as I ask you."

So he took out the statue's other eye, and darted down with it. He swooped past the match-girl, and slipped the jewel into the palm of her hand. "What a lovely bit of glass," said the little girl; and she ran home laughing.

Then the Swallow came back to the Happy Prince. "You are blind now," he said, "so I will stay with you always."

"No, little Swallow," said the Prince, "you must go away to the warm lands."

"I will stay with you always," said the Swallow, and he slept at the Happy Prince's feet.

All the next day he sat on the Prince's shoulder, and told him stories of what he had seen in strange lands. He told him of the red birds who catch fish in their beaks; of the great green snake that sleeps in a palm tree, and has twenty priests to feed it with honey-cakes; and of the little folk who sail over a big lake on large flat leaves, and are always at war with the butterflies.

"Dear little Swallow," said the Prince, "you tell me of amazing things, but more amazing than anything is the suffering of men and women. Fly over my city, little Swallow, and tell me what you see there."

So the Swallow flew over the great city, and saw the rich making merry in their great houses, while the beggars were sitting at their gates. He flew into dark lanes and saw the white faces of starving children looking out at the black streets.

Under the archway of a bridge two little boys were lying in one another's arms, to try and keep themselves warm. "How hungry we are!" they said. "You must not lie here!" shouted the watchman, and they walked out into the rain.

Then the Swallow flew back and told the Prince what he had seen.

"I am covered with fine gold," said the statue, "you must take it off, leaf by leaf, and give it to my poor; the living always think that gold can make them happy."

Leaf after leaf of fine gold the Swallow picked off, till the Happy Prince looked quite dull and grey. Leaf after leaf of fine gold he brought to the poor, and the children's faces grew rosier; and they laughed and played games in the street.

"We have bread now!" they laughed.

Then the snow came, and after the snow came the frost. The streets looked as if they were made of silver, they were so bright and glistening. Everybody went about in furs, and the little boys wore scarlet caps and skated on the ice.

146

The poor little Swallow grew colder and colder, but he would not leave the Prince; he loved him so well. He picked up crumbs outside the baker's door when the baker was not looking, and tried to keep himself warm by flapping his wings.

But at last he knew that he was going to die. He had just enough strength to fly up to the Prince's shoulder once more. "Goodbye, dear Prince," he murmured, "will you let me kiss your hand."

"I am glad that you are going to the warm lands at last, little Swallow," said the Prince, "you have stayed here too long; but you must kiss me on the lips, for I love you."

"It is not to the warm lands that I am going," said the Swallow. "I am going to the House of Death. Death is the Brother of Sleep, is he not?"

And he kissed the Happy Prince on the lips, and fell down dead at his feet.

At that moment a curious crack sounded inside the statue, as if something had broken. The fact is that the leaden heart had snapped right in two. It certainly was a dreadfully hard frost.

147

Early next morning the Mayor was walking in the square below with the Town Councillors. As they passed the column he looked up at the statue. "Dear me! how shabby the Happy Prince looks!" he said.

"How shabby indeed!" cried the Town Councillors, who always agreed with the Mayor; and they went up to look at it.

"The ruby has fallen out of his sword, his eyes are gone, and he is golden no longer," said the Mayor; "in fact he is little better than a beggar!"

"Little better than a beggar!" said the Town Councillors.

"And here is a dead bird at our feet," said the Mayor. "Birds should not be allowed to die here."

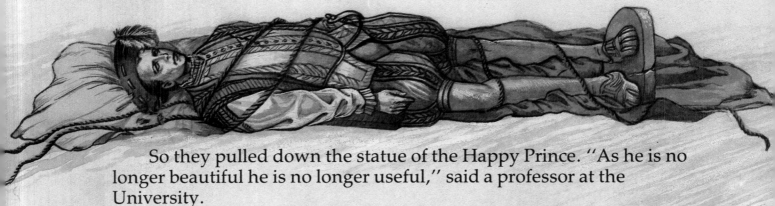

So they pulled down the statue of the Happy Prince. "As he is no longer beautiful he is no longer useful," said a professor at the University.

Then they melted the statue in a furnace, and the Mayor held a meeting of the Councillors to decide what was to be done with the metal. "We must have another statue, of course," he said, "and it shall be a statue of myself."

"Of myself," said each of the Town Councillors, and they quarrelled. When I last heard of them they were quarrelling still.

"What a strange thing," said the foreman in charge of the workmen at the furnace. "The broken lead heart will not melt in the heat. We must throw it away." So they threw it on a dust-heap where the dead Swallow was also lying.

"Bring me the two most precious things in the city," said God to one of his Angels; and the Angel brought Him the leaden heart and the dead bird.

"You have rightly chosen," said God, "for in my garden of Paradise this little bird shall sing for evermore, and in my city of gold the Happy Prince shall praise me."

THE TRAVELS OF BARON MUNCHAUSEN

by Rudolph Raspe

There are some who say that I exaggerate too much and that the tales of my life cannot be believed. I say in return that my life has been so exciting that I have had adventures beyond the belief of those who stay at home. Many of these great doings seem to have been concerned with animals.

When I was still a young man I visited the island of Ceylon and went out on a shooting expedition. Near the banks of a large piece of water I heard a rustling noise behind me. I turned to see a lion advancing upon me. My musket was filled only with pellets for shooting birds, and would have no effect on this beast. I was sure that my end had come.

I turned to flee. The moment I turned about I saw a large crocodile coming out of the water towards me, his mouth wide open.

I fell to the ground in fear. At that very moment the lion sprang at me. I lay expecting at any moment to feel his teeth tearing at me. Nothing happened. I raised my head. To my great joy I saw that the lion had soared right over my form and had dived down the throat of the waiting crocodile. The latter half of his body was sticking out of the crocodile's mouth. As I watched, the lion suffocated and the crocodile choked to death. When my companions found me I was standing proudly over the two dead bodies.

Some years later I was travelling in the frozen land of Russia in the middle of a dreadful winter. On my way across the snows I passed what I took to be a poor peasant lying on the ground, freezing to death. I took pity on the poor fellow and dropped my cloak over him before riding on. As I did so, I heard the man's voice calling after me,

"You will be given a great reward for this kindness!"

I rode on until night fell, meeting no one else on my journey. I became very tired and dismounted to sleep. In front of me, sticking out of the snow, was something like the pointed stump of a tree. I tied the reins of my horse to this to prevent him from wandering away in the night. Then I fell asleep.

The next morning, when I woke up, I found that I was lying on the ground in a churchyard on the edge of a village. I could see my horse nowhere. Then I heard him neigh above my head. I looked upwards. There he was, hanging by his reins from the steeple of the church!

I realised what had happened. The whole village had been covered with snow to a great depth in the storm the previous day. The snow had been piled so high that it had almost covered the church steeple, all except the tiny part which I had seen and to which I had tied my mount.

During the night, while I had been sleeping so soundly, much of the snow beneath me had melted, carrying me gently down to the ground. My poor horse, on the other hand, had remained tied to the steeple.

Fortunately getting the mount down presented no problem. I picked up one of my pistols, took aim and fired. My shot broke the reins and the horse fell to earth, landing in a pile of soft snow. I repaired the reins, mounted and rode off.

My poor horse had escaped this time, but it was not long before he met his end. The snow underfoot had become so thick that I had tied a sledge to my horse and was being dragged along on this sledge by my mount through a dreadful forest. Suddenly a large wolf leapt out of the trees and gave chase. My horse pulled me away on the sledge as fast as he could, but it was not long before the wolf caught up with us. He leapt clean over the sledge and fell upon the hind-quarters of my horse, starting to swallow and eat my mount.

I raised my head and saw to my horror what was happening. In an effort to help the horse I started hitting the wolf with my whip. This unexpected attack from the rear so frightened the wolf that he leapt forward with all his might. The carcase of the dead horse fell to the ground, but by this time the wolf was caught up in the harness, and could not free himself. He was now pulling the sledge instead of the horse, and by using my reins and my whip I was able to control him until we reached the next town, where I shot the wolf and bought a new horse.

In order to obtain food on my travels I depended a great deal on my skill as a hunter, and some of my expeditions in the large forests in search of food were responsible for one or two incredible adventures.

Once I came across a great wild boar, with two enormous curved tusks. I fired and missed. There was no time to reload, so I ran and hid behind a tree.
Almost blind with rage the boar charged at the tree concealing me. He hit it with a tremendous shock, and his tusks became embedded deep in the trunk of the tree, holding him fast.

Cautiously I emerged from my hiding place. The boar struggled and squealed, but he was held fast by his own sharp tusks. I picked up a large stone and hammered away at those tusks until they were so bent that there was no possible chance of the boar releasing himself from the tree. Then I went off to fetch a horse and cart with which to pick up my prisoner.

It was in the same vast forest that I had my strange encounter with a stag. He was a noble beast, with great antlers growing out of his head. I raised my musket to fire at him, and then realised that I had used up all my ammunition, leaving only a small supply of powder.

Then I remembered that for my lunch I had eaten a handful of cherries. Not wishing to litter the ground with my rubbish I had placed the stones in my pocket. I took these out now and put them in my musket, along with the gunpowder. Taking careful aim I fired the stones at the stag. As usual my aim was perfect.

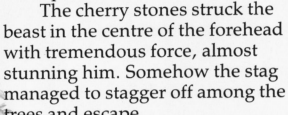

The cherry stones struck the beast in the centre of the forehead with tremendous force, almost stunning him. Somehow the stag managed to stagger off among the trees and escape.

A year later I was hunting with some friends in that same part of the forest. Out came the stag I had fired at twelve months before. I recognised him at once, for growing out of the middle of his forehead, where my cherry stones had struck him, was a fine cherry tree. I shot the beast, skinned it, cooked the meat and ate it with some cherry sauce made from the tree that had been growing out of its head.

In the course of my life I had some strange experiences with tame animals as well as with wild ones. Once, I remember, I owned a greyhound. This was the swiftest dog I ever knew, and he never lost a race. Unfortunately in these races he ran so fast that over the years he quite wore down his legs, until in the end they were no longer than those of a dachshund. Naturally I had to retire the animal as a racing dog, and keep him as a pet, and for many years more he would scurry around after me on his tiny legs.

My favourite horse Ajax also had his share of marvellous adventures. Once I rode him into battle against the Turks when I was in command of a fine body of soldiers. One day we came across a body of mounted Turks and attacked them so bravely that the Turks and their horses soon turned and fled. Of course my men and I rode after them as fast as we could go. Ajax was much faster than any other horse in my command, and we soon out-distanced the rest of my soldiers, so that I was chasing those Turks on my own.

I followed them until they reached their fortress, and even went in after them when their guards raised the portcullis, the gate with the huge sharp spikes in the fortress wall.

Once I was in the yard of the fortress, however, I realised that I was on my own, and that even I could not defeat the entire Turkish force without the aid of my soldiers. I at once turned Ajax and rode out of the yard. As I did so, the Turks brought the portcullis down hard behind me in an attempt to trap me.

I rode back swiftly until I reached the nearest friendly town. There I decided to wait until the rest of my men caught up with me. In the meantime, I decided Ajax must be thirsty after all his hard riding, so I rode him over to a pond in the town square, remaining on his back while he drank his fill.

That poor beast drank and drank until the pond was drained. I was amazed. Then I heard the sound of water running away behind me. I turned in my saddle and gazed back. To my astonishment I saw that the entire rear part of the horse had been cut off by the portcullis as it had fallen behind me. I had been riding the fore-part of the steed only. Of course that meant that the water was just pouring out of the beast as soon as he drank it!

I was very relieved when, at this moment, the rest of my men joined me. I was able to send several of them to the Turks' fortress, where they picked up the rear portion of my mount and brought it back to me.

One of the grooms in my force had some skill with a needle, and he was able to sew the two parts of Ajax back together. For this purpose, instead of thread he used young shoots of a laurel bush. Later on, after the wound had healed, these shoots took root inside Ajax's body. After a time these grew up over his back in the form of a leafy arch, so that even in the hottest weather I was able to ride in the shade.

It was not only on land that I encountered strange creatures. Once, while travelling by sea, I had the misfortune to be swallowed by a whale.

It was a fine day off the coast of France, and while our ship was at anchor I took the chance to dive over the side for a pleasant swim. No sooner had I entered the water than I saw this great whale bearing down on me, his jaws opened wide. In a second he had swallowed me.

It was dark and warm in the stomach of the whale, but I decided that I did not really want to stay there. I set about causing the creature as much pain as possible, so that he would be glad to throw me back up into the sea. Accordingly I danced and jumped as heavily as I could. None of my movements, however, seemed to disturb him, for the great whale kept on cruising calmly on, while I tired myself out in his great stomach.

Then I had one of those strokes of fortune which have followed me all through my life. An Italian ship, hunting whales, came across my captor. They followed him and speared him to death with their harpoons. This they followed by hauling the great creature up on to the deck of their ship, while I remained a prisoner in the stomach of the dead beast.

154

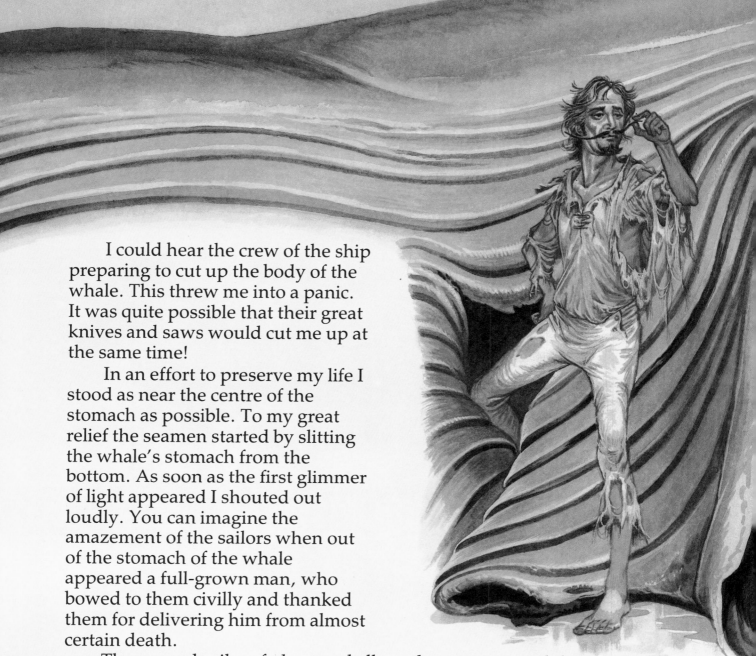

I could hear the crew of the ship preparing to cut up the body of the whale. This threw me into a panic. It was quite possible that their great knives and saws would cut me up at the same time!

In an effort to preserve my life I stood as near the centre of the stomach as possible. To my great relief the seamen started by slitting the whale's stomach from the bottom. As soon as the first glimmer of light appeared I shouted out loudly. You can imagine the amazement of the sailors when out of the stomach of the whale appeared a full-grown man, who bowed to them civilly and thanked them for delivering him from almost certain death.

Those good sailors fed me and allowed me to rest, and then took me back to the vessel on which I had been sailing. As far as I can tell, I was in the whale's stomach for almost five hours.

From the sunny seas off the shores of France the vessel took me, in good time, to the frozen seas of the great northern waters. While sailing past many icebergs one day, I saw through my telescope a large white polar bear. We were very short of meat so I had myself set aground on the iceberg. I then approached the great bear and shot it.

Unfortunately the report of my musket alerted thousands of bears who had been asleep on the ice. I could see them approaching in the distance, and knew that unless I thought of something quickly my last moment would soon be at hand.

Swiftly I took my hunting knife from my belt. With a few swift strokes I skinned the bear I had shot, kicking the carcase of the dead bear through a hole in the ice. I then wrapped the skin of the bear around me, putting my head under the bear's.

Soon all the other bears came nosing up to me, sniffing at my fur and touching me gently with their paws. Evidently they took me for the one I had shot, because they seemed to accept me as one of themselves. For my part I imitated their actions as best I could, until the time came that night for me to slip away from the others and get back to the small boat, in which I rowed thankfully back to the vessel.

As it happened, I got home from that voyage not by sea, as I had left, but by air. It happened in this way. I had gone ashore again one day and had climbed a tall hill. At the top of this hill was a large hole. I stood astride the hole and idly dropped a stone into it. I was not aware of this, but there was an eagle at the bottom of the hole. My stone disturbed her so greatly that she flew out of the hole in a great flurry. As I was standing astride the hole as she came out, the eagle bore me away with her on her back.

We flew for many days in this fashion, pausing to rest at night. Unfortunately for me, each time that the eagle stopped to rest it was on the top of a high mountain, so that I could not escape, but had to get on her back the next day in order to continue my journey.

I lost all count of time, but set my mind to overcoming my problem. After a great deal of thought I discovered that by pulling at the eagle's head I could change the direction in which she was flying. I plotted a course by the stars, and in this way got her to take me quite close to my home and to land me on a flat piece of land, before she flew off again.